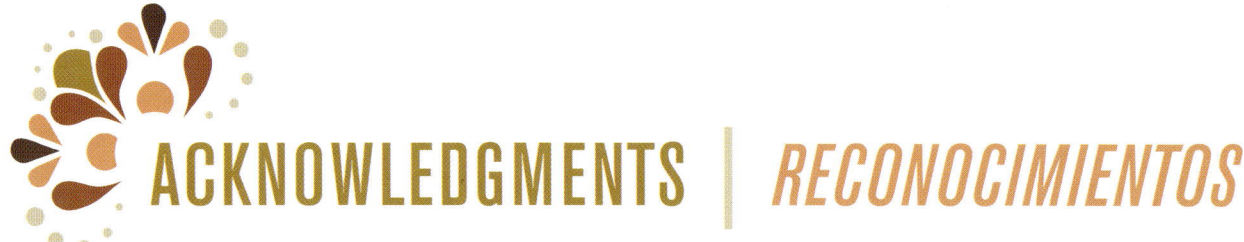

ACKNOWLEDGMENTS | *RECONOCIMIENTOS*

Published by Louisiana State University Museum of Art
Distributed by Louisiana State University Press
Copyright ©2015 Louisiana State University Museum of Art
All rights reserved

Louisiana State University Museum of Art
Shaw Center for the Arts, 5th Floor
100 Lafayette Street
Baton Rouge, LA 70801
www.lsumoa.com

ISBN: 978-0-8071-6334-4

This book is published by Louisiana State University Museum of Art in conjunction with the exhibition *Mexico in New Orleans: A Tale of Two Americas,* May 5 –August 30, 2015.

This catalogue was made possible through the generous support of Linda and Robert Bowsher, whose passion for art history helped inspire this catalogue and exhibition. Thank you to Belinda Flores Shinshillas and the Mexican Consulate of New Orleans for the elegant Spanish language translation, and to Don Fuson for supporting catalogue photography and research. The Historic New Orleans Collection, The Latin American Library at Tulane University, The LSU Textile and Costume Museum, The Meadows Museum of Art, Dr. Tlaloc Alferez, H.P. and Barbara Bacot, John Edward Bradley, Shanna Boudreaux, Natalie Fielding, Don Fuson, Olive Leonhardt, Penny Morrill, Caroline Wogan and Stephen Louis Sontheimer and Ann Wilkinson all contributed key works of art to the exhibition and helped facilitate catalogue research and photography. Special thanks go to H.P. Bacot, Judith H. Bonner, Hortensia Calvo, Merrill Domas, Don Fuson, Randy Harelson, Christine Hernandez, John Lawrence, Gay Leonhardt, Penny Morrill, Lisa Nicoletti and Pamela Rabalais-Vinci for invaluable research advice and consultations. Thank you to the LSU Graphic Design Student Office, and especially Kitty Pheney, Juan Baldera and Luisa F. Restrepo Pérez for designing a beautiful catalogue, and to Fran Huber, Lucy Perera, Tanya Anderson, Rodneyna Hart, Rebecca Abadie, Kim Jones and Brooke Storey at the LSU Museum of Art for their hard work and passion for this project.

Curated by Katie A. Pfohl

Text by Katie A. Pfohl   Spanish Translation by Belinda Flores Shinshillas

Design and Production:

Producer: Kitty Pheney   **Creative Director:** Luisa Fernanda Restrepo Pérez
Faculty Advisors: Lynne Baggett & Rod Parker   **Designers:** Juan Baldera & Luisa Fernanda Restrepo Pérez

LSU School of Art: Graphic Design Student Office
Photography: Katie A. Pfohl
Printing: IPC Printing, Baton Rouge, LA

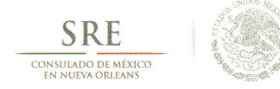 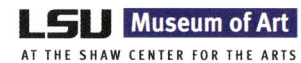 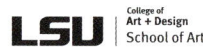 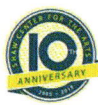

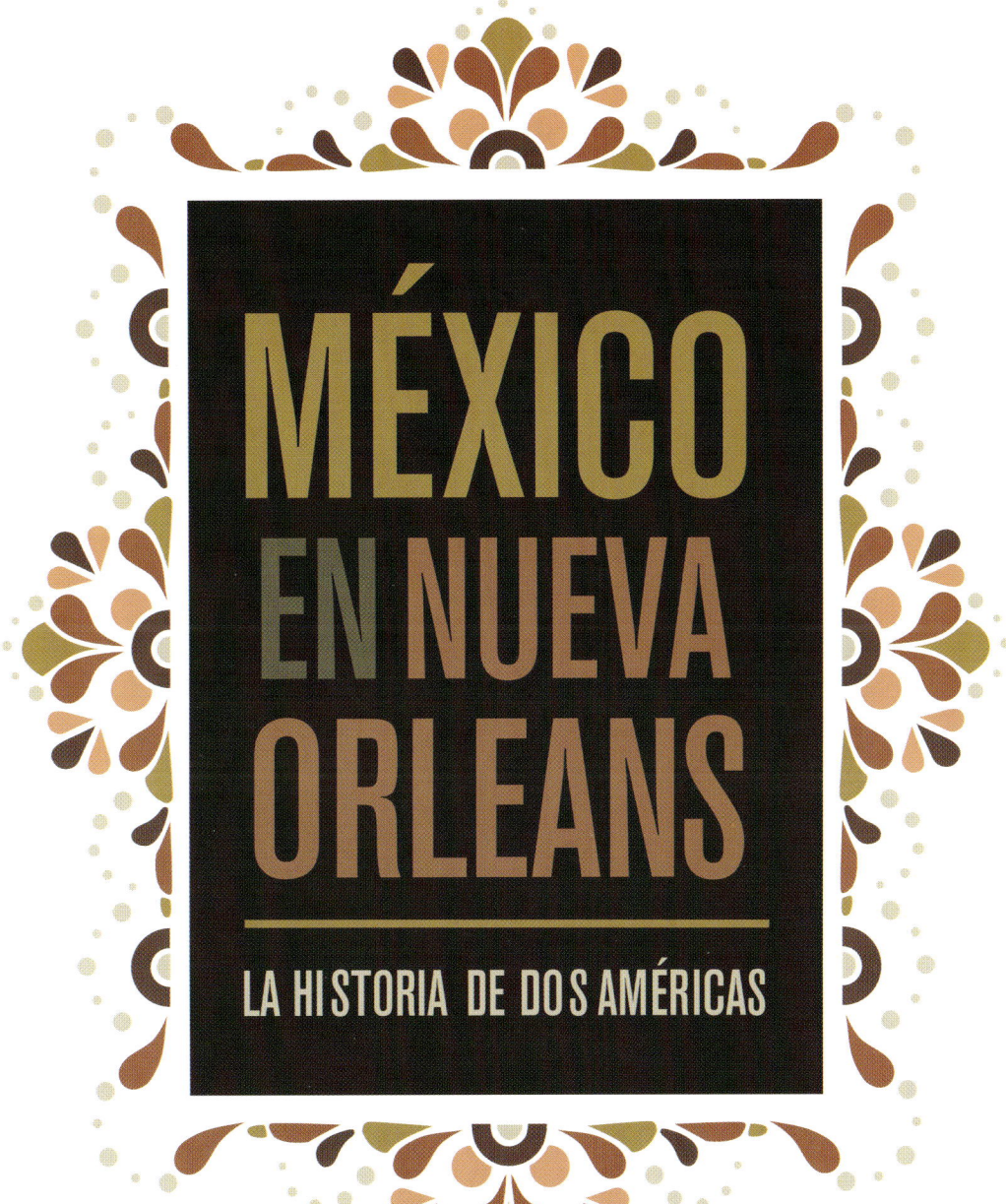

MÉXICO EN NUEVA ORLEANS

LA HISTORIA DE DOS AMÉRICAS

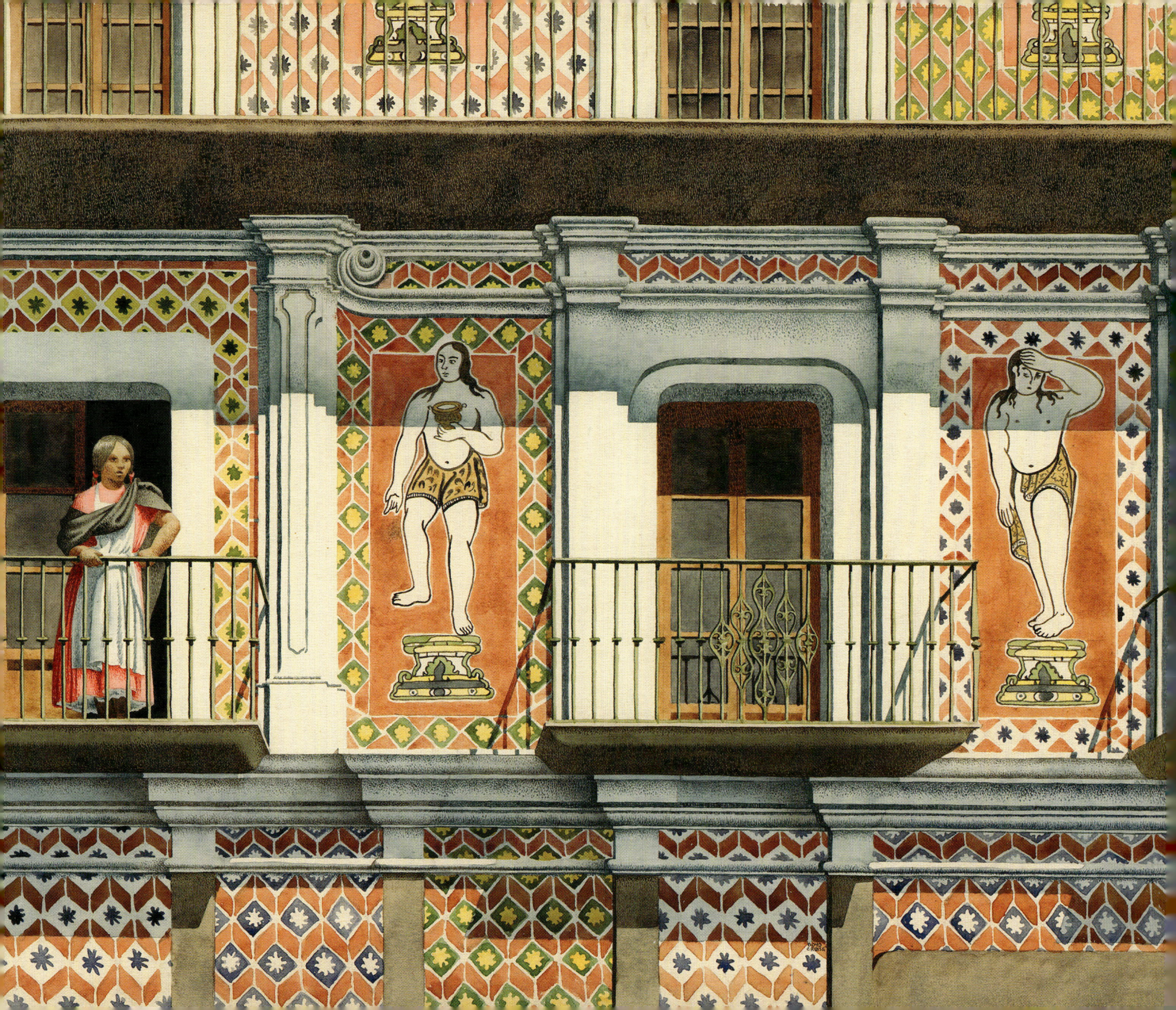

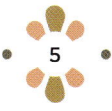

MEXICO IN NEW ORLEANS:
A Tale Of Two Americas

Text by Katie A. Pfohl

MÉXICO EN NUEVA ORLEANS:
La Historia De Dos Américas

Spanish Translation by Belinda Flores Shinshillas

From the 1920s through 1950s, Louisiana artists and writers flocked to Mexico, lured by descriptions of the place as a new "Land of Promise."[1] In the wake of the Mexican Revolution, Mexico swarmed with Louisiana artists and intellectuals seeking respite from the Great Depression and exposure to the bold and politically provocative new art coming out of Mexico.[2] The 1920s marked the beginning of a period of particularly vibrant cultural and artistic connections between the two regions as New Orleans artists began travelling to Mexico en masse to experience its dynamic art and culture, which they viewed as closely connected to the culture and spirit of New Orleans.

In the 1920s, New Orleans artists like William Spratling and Caroline Durieux travelled to Mexico to learn from masters of Mexican modern art like Diego Rivera, Emilio Amero, and Carlos Orozco Romero, and to study the Pre-Columbian and Mesoamerican art from which these artists derived much of their inspiration. To them, modern Mexican art represented a fusion between past and present that had much to teach Louisiana artists searching for a form of modern art still tied to the rich international history and culture of New Orleans—an art that, in the words of anthropologist Frances Toor, could express "the present in relationship to the past and future."[3]

In the early 1920s, Tulane University archaeologist and adventurer Frans Blom captivated Louisianans with his new discoveries about ancient Pre-Columbian and Mesoamerican art and culture. Newspapers and magazines ran enthralling accounts of his ambitious archaeological excavations of Mayan ruins and explorations of the Isthmus of Tehuantepec. Blom pitched his archaeological projects to the Louisiana populace as providing "information useful to the Port of New Orleans"

Desde la década de 1920 hasta 1950, artistas y escritores del Estado de Luisiana visitaron México, atraídos por las descripciones del lugar como una nueva "tierra prometida"[1]. En el despertar después de la Revolución Mexicana, México se vio colmado de artistas e intelectuales de Luisiana que buscaban un respiro a la Gran Depresión y así tener un acercamiento al nuevo arte, audaz y políticamente provocativo, que se desarrollaba en México.[2] La década de 1920 marcó el comienzo de un período de importantes conexiones culturales y artísticas entre las dos regiones, cuando artistas de Nueva Orleans comenzaron a viajar a México para ser parte de la experiencia y dinámica de su arte y cultura, la cual consideraban estrechamente relacionada con la de Nueva Orleans.

En la década de 1920, artistas de Nueva Orleans como William Spratling y Caroline Durieux empezaron a viajar a México para aprender de los maestros del arte moderno mexicano como Diego Rivera, Emilio Amero y Carlos Orozco Romero. Así como para estudiar el arte precolombino y de mesoamericana, los cuales representan una gran parte de su inspiración. Para ellos, el arte moderno mexicano representó una fusión entre el pasado y el presente que tenía mucho que mostrar a los artistas de Luisiana, en la búsqueda de una forma de arte moderno, arraigado a la rica historia y cultura internacional de Nueva Orleans, un arte que, en palabras del antropólogo Frances Toor, podía expresar "el presente en relación con el pasado y el futuro."[3]

A principios de la década de 1920, el arqueólogo y aventurero de la Universidad de Tulane Frans Blom cautivó a la gente de Luisiana con sus nuevos descubrimientos sobre el arte antiguo, la cultura precolombina y mesoamericana. Periódicos y revistas narraron historias apasionantes de sus ambiciosas excavaciones arqueológicas de las ruinas Mayas y

Boyd Cruise
Casa de los Muñecos/House of Dolls, 1954
Watercolor on paper
The Historic New Orleans Collection, 1956.20

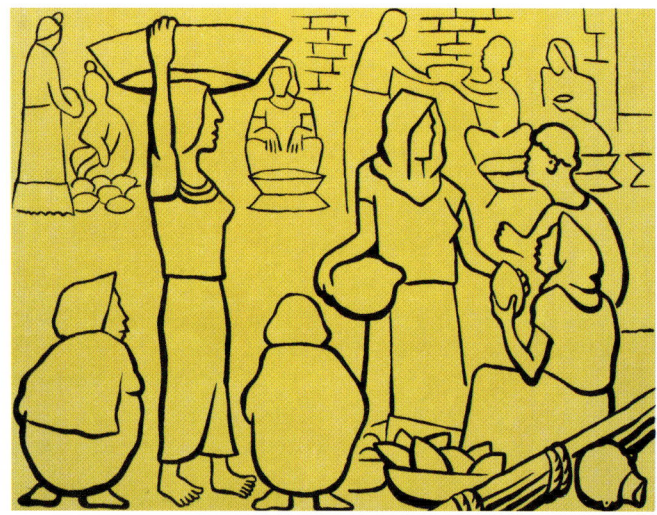

as the city expanded its international reach into Mexico, and continually highlighted the cultural and artistic connections between the two regions.[4]

Blom's enthralling explorations of ancient art and architecture encouraged many of his New Orleans artist friends to follow in his footsteps to Mexico. In the late 1920s, Blom's friend William Spratling joined him in Mexico with plans to conduct a detailed study of Pre-Columbian art and architecture and write a travelogue about his time in the country.[5] Spratling's time in Mexico altered the course of his entire career, inspiring him to move to Taxco to become one of the strongest voices in the revival of the Mexican silversmithing tradition.

By 1931, Spratling had opened his own silver shop adjacent to the region's famed silver mines, creating strikingly modern silver designs inspired by Pre-Columbian art and patterns, often in collaboration with other Mexican artists and artisans.[6] Like many Mexican artists of the time, Spratling saw in the striking graphic forms and strong geometric

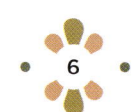

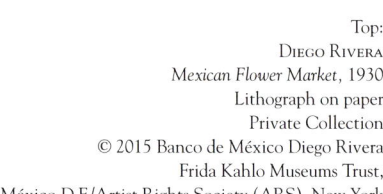

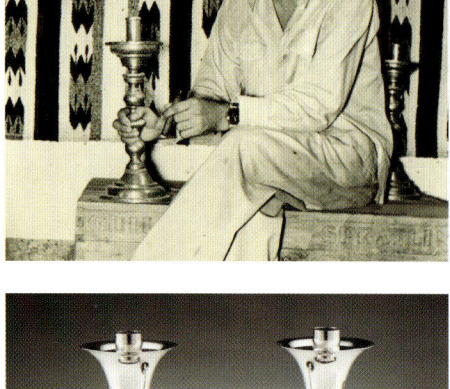

Top:
Diego Rivera
Mexican Flower Market, 1930
Lithograph on paper
Private Collection
© 2015 Banco de México Diego Rivera
Frida Kahlo Museums Trust,
México D.F./Artist Rights Society (ARS), New York

Center:
*Photograph of William Spratling
Holding one of his Candlesticks*, c. 1940s
Silver Gelatin Print
The Latin American Library, Tulane University
Spratling-Taxco Collection
Photo © David Humphreys, 2015

Bottom:
William Spratling
Candlesticks, c. 1940s
Wood and silver
Collection of Don Fuson

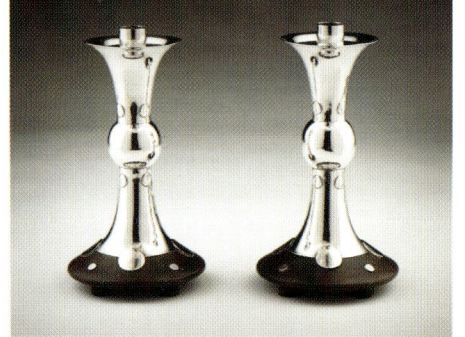

exploraciones del Istmo de Tehuantepec. Blom mostró sus proyectos arqueológicos a la población de Luisiana para proporcionar "información útil para el puerto de Nueva Orleans", cuando esta ciudad expandió su lazos internacionales en México y continuamente destacó los vínculos culturales y artísticos entre las dos regiones.[4]

Las exploraciones fascinantes de Blom del arte y la arquitectura antigua alentaron a muchos de sus amigos artistas de Nueva Orleans a seguir sus pasos en México. A finales de 1920, William Spratling, amigo de Blom, se reunió con él en México con planes de realizar un estudio detallado sobre el arte precolombino y su arquitectura, para poder escribir un diario sobre su viaje en el país.[5] El tiempo que Spratling pasó en México alteró el curso de toda su carrera, lo inspiró a ir a Taxco para convertirse en una de las voces más fuertes en el renacimiento de la tradición de la platería mexicana.

En 1931, Spratling había abierto su propio taller de platería junto a las famosas minas de plata de la región, para dedicarse a la creación de diseños sorprendentemente modernos inspirados en el arte precolombino, a menudo diseñados en colaboración con otros artistas y artesanos mexicanos.[6] Al igual que muchos artistas mexicanos de la época, Spratling vio en las

shapes of Pre-Columbian art inspiration for a new form of modern art—a way of modernizing while still maintaining ties to past tradition.

Spratling filled his 1932 travelogue *Little Mexico* with illustrations of contemporary Mexican scenes whose forms recall the Pre-Columbian clay seal stamp imprints he would have encountered on Blom's archaeological digs, as well as the jewelry and decorative arts he would later design. So doing, Spratling sought to create visual ties between Mexico's past art and its present-day landscapes and peoples, creating what his architect friend Carlos Obregon called "a Mexican style of our times which the country's ancient civilization has not impeded and in which it may be perpetuated."[7] In his foreword to *Little Mexico,* the Mexican artist Diego Rivera praised Spratling's book as "a portrait of Mexico composed of many small portraits of people and things," writing that Spratling's small portraits of Mexico had "the acuteness and grace of those painted by certain masters in my country who died before I was born."[8]

formas geométricas del arte Precolombino inspiración para una nueva forma de arte, una innovadora forma de modernización, manteniendo lazos con la tradición del pasado.

Spratling ilustró en 1932 su libro de viajero Little Mexico *con litografías de escenas contemporáneas mexicanas, cuyas formas hacían recordar los sellos de arcillas precolombinas que se habían encontrado en las excavaciones arqueológicas de Blom, así como las joyas y arte decorativo que él diseñaría más adelante. En esta práctica, Spratling buscó crear vínculos visuales entre el arte del pasado de México y sus paisajes modernos, creando lo que su amigo, el arquitecto Carlos Obregón, llamó "un estilo mexicano de nuestro tiempo que la civilización y tradición antigua del país no ha impedido, y que puede ser eternizado."[7] En su prólogo a* Little México, *el artista mexicano Diego Rivera elogió el libro de Spratling como "Un retrato de México, compuesto de muchos pequeños retratos de personas y cosas," el escrito de pequeños retratos de Spratling tenía "la gravedad y la gracia de lo pintado por ciertos maestros en mi país (México) que murieron antes de que yo naciera."[8]*

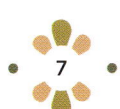

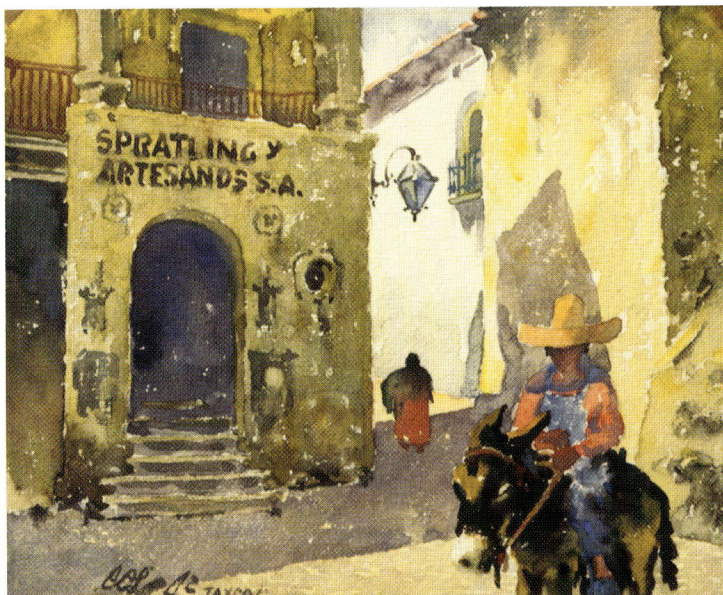

Charles Oglesby Longabaugh
Spratling y Artesanos, u.d.
Watercolor on paper
The Latin American Library, Tulane University
Spratling-Taxco Collection

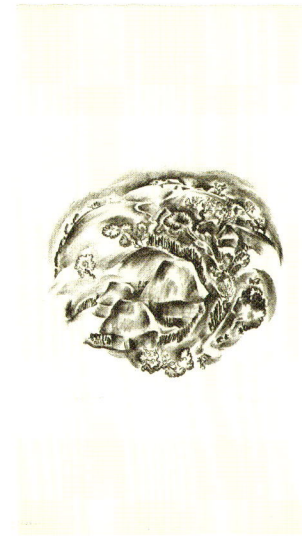
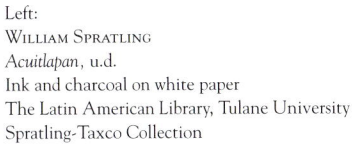

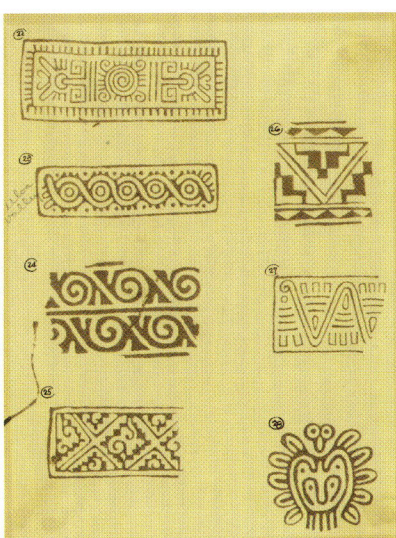

Left:
William Spratling
Acuitlapan, u.d.
Ink and charcoal on white paper
The Latin American Library, Tulane University
Spratling-Taxco Collection

Right:
William Spratling
Pre-Columbian Clay Seal Stamp Imprints 22-28, u.d.
Photostatic copy on paper
The Latin American Library, Tulane University
Spratling-Taxco Collection

For Spratling, modern Mexican art inspired not just on the level of form and composition, but also in its capacity to make profound political statements. In 1931, Spratling wrote a passionate introduction to the Mexican artist David Alfaro Siqueiros' book *13 Grabados,* a series of 13 woodcut prints that Siqueiros published to document his imprisonment in Mexico as a political dissident in the late 1920s. In his introduction, Spratling praised Siqueiros' woodcuts for an economy of form that Spratling saw as connected to the bold, graphic patterns of Pre-Columbian art. Through the "simplicity and power of his use of form and color," Spratling wrote, Siqueiros arrived at a "cumulative force of facts" about his time in prison that made this work into a bold and daring political statement. Modern Mexican art, Spratling concluded, was "the only great new school of art since the Flemish School."[9]

To Rivera, Spratling, and many of the other artists and writers working between Mexico and New Orleans, indigenous Mexican art offered a much more powerful precedent for a new art of the South than European tradition. The bold, graphic forms of Pre-Columbian art not

Para Spratling, el arte moderno mexicano no inspiraba sólo en el nivel de la forma y la composición, sino también en su capacidad de hacer declaraciones políticas profundas. En 1931, Spratling escribió una introducción apasionada sobre el libro del artista David Alfaro Siqueiros "13 Grabados", el cual comprendía una serie de 13 grabados en madera que Siqueiros publicó para documentar su encarcelamiento en México por disidente político a finales de 1920. En esta introducción, Spratling elogió en estos grabados, la forma económica que Siqueiros utilizó, y que Spratling vio como una conexión con los diseños llamativos de la gráfica del arte precolombino. A través de la " sencillez y el poder del uso de la forma y color ", escribió Spratling, "Siqueiros llegó a una fuerza acumulativa de hechos", durante su tiempo en prisión y que hizo que este trabajo fuera una declaración política audaz y atrevida. Spratling llegó a la conclusión de que el arte moderno mexicano, era "la única nueva y grandiosa escuela de arte desde la escuela flamenca."[9]

Para Rivera, el arte indígena mexicano ofreció un precedente mucho más potente para Spratling y para muchos de los otros artistas y escritores que trabajan entre México y Nueva Orleans, que la tradición europea,

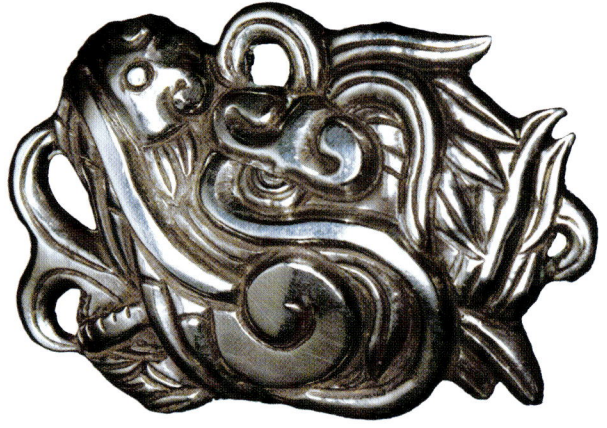

WILLIAM SPRATLING
Quetzalcoatl brooch, c. 1940
Silver
Collection of Penny Morrill

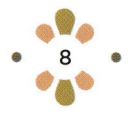

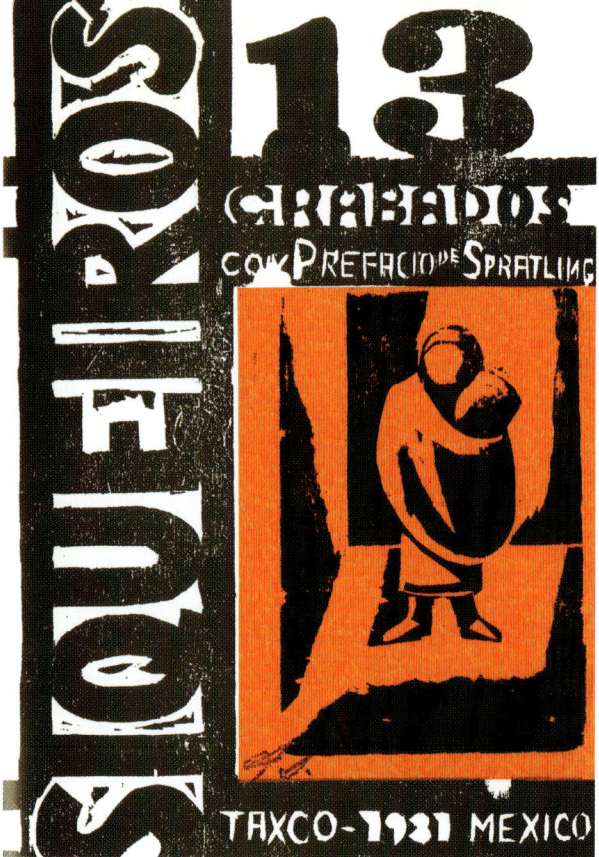

only more closely resembled modern art, but were also more closely tied to the indigenous culture that artists like Spratling and Rivera sought to champion and support. In a 1930 article for the bilingual journal *Mexican Folkways,* Rivera continually discouraged Mexican and American artists from imitating European art, writing that the authentic character of art in both Mexico and the United States was "clouded, hidden, and frequently destroyed by imitation of one or more European painters."[10] In 1930, a critic for *The Times-Picayune* likewise urged Louisiana artists to turn their gaze from the art of Europe and towards the art of Mexico, writing that Mexican art was "more nearly related to us emotionally" than European art.[11]

Spratling, like Rivera and other Mexican artists of the time, saw many "parallel sympathies and shared ideas" between Mexican and American— and particularly Louisianan—artists. In a 1930 article about Rivera's work, Spratling compared Rivera's artistic sensibilities to those of the New Orleans writer Sherwood Anderson, whose 1925 novel *Dark Laughter* seemed to Spratling to share Rivera's deep fascination with history,

para crear un nuevo arte del Sur. Las formas graficas audaces del arte precolombino no sólo eran más cercanas al arte moderno, pero también estaban más estrechamente ligadas a la cultura indígena, artistas como Spratling y Rivera vieron esto como un estandarte y apoyo. En un artículo de 1930 de la revista bilingüe Mexican Folkways, *Rivera desalentado ante la continua imitación de artistas mexicanos y estadounidenses del arte europeo, escribió que el carácter auténtico de arte, tanto en México como en Estados Unidos estaba "nublado, escondido, y frecuentemente destruido por la imitación de uno o más pintores europeos".[10] Asimismo, en 1930 un crítico del* Times-Picayune *incitó a artistas de Luisiana a dirigir su mirada hacia el arte de México, escribiendo que el arte mexicano estaba "más emocionalmente cercano y relacionado con nosotros "que el arte europeo.[11]*

Spratling, como Rivera y otros artistas mexicanos de la época, vieron muchas "similitudes paralelas e ideas compartidas" entre artistas mexicanos y estadounidenses, y en particular artistas de Luisiana. En un artículo de 1930 sobre el trabajo de Rivera, Spratling comparó la sensibilidad artística de Rivera a la del escritor de Nueva Orleans Sherwood Anderson, cuya novela "La risa oscura" publicada en 1925 le parecía a Spratling que

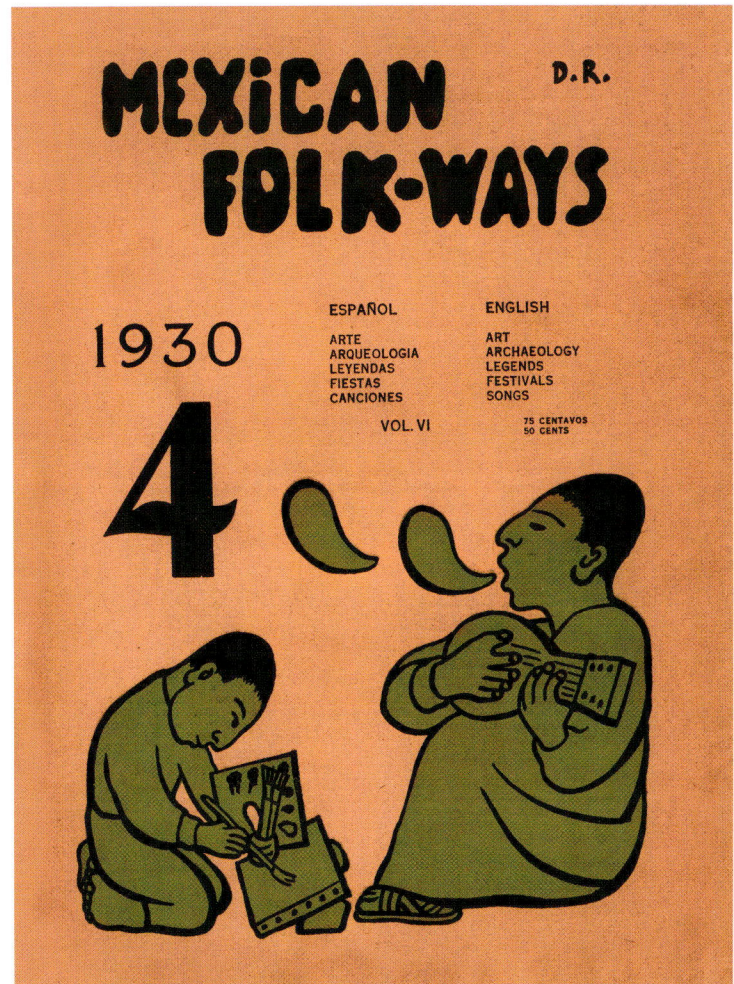

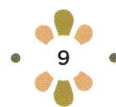

Cover of Mexican Folkways, 1930
The Latin American Library, Tulane University

Opposite:
DAVID ALFARO SIQUEIROS
Cover of 13 Grabados en Madera por Siqueiros, Taxco, 1931 (printed 1992)
Portfolio of 13 woodcuts (12 printed on orange paper and one printed on lavender paper)
The Latin American Library, Tulane University, Spratling-Taxco Collection, MSS Collection 148,
© 2015 Artists Rights Society (ARS), New York / SOMAAP, Mexico City

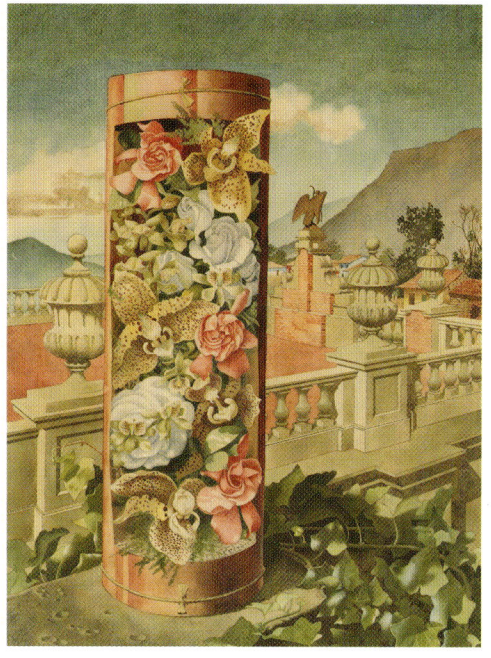

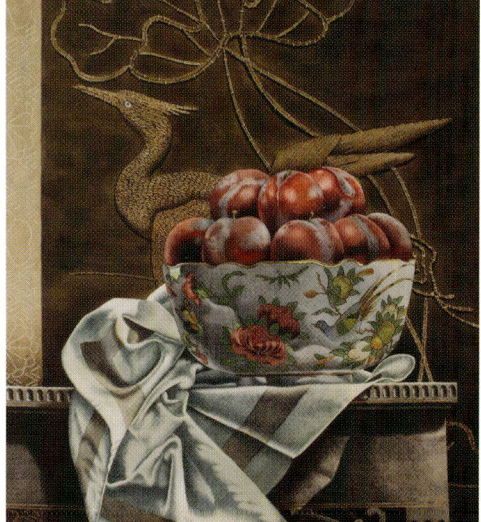

biting satirical sensibility, and penchant for social and political critique.[12] Rivera, Spratling wrote, "belong[ed] not only to his epoch in Mexico, but [had] achieved a sort of internationalism." In Rivera's work, Spratling saw the potential to create cultural connections between North America and South America that could unite the two regions and bring American art more in line with what Rivera called "the living tradition of the land of the South."[13]

In 1927, the New Orleans Arts and Crafts Club mounted an exhibition of Spratling's Mexican architectural drawings that featured Spratling's work from Mexico alongside his architectural sketches of the French Quarter. *The Times Picayune* review of Spratling's exhibition commented on the strong visual similarities between Spratling's sketches of Mexico and his sketches of New Orleans, noting that the images of Mexico and of Louisiana were "held together by a considerable unity," and characterizing both the Mexican and Louisianan images as "Southern scenes," whether they originated in "the United States or in its neighbor Mexico."[14] During this period, the Mexican and Louisianan

compartía la profunda fascinación de Rivera con la historia, de sensibilidad satírica, así como su gusto por la crítica social y política.[12] Spratling escribió Spratling escribió " Rivera, pertenece no sólo a su época en México, pero ha logrado una especie de internacionalismo." En la obra de Rivera, Spratling vio el potencial para crear conexiones culturales entre América del Norte y América del Sur, misma que podría unir las dos regiones y acercar el arte americano más a la línea que Rivera llamó "la tradición viva de la tierra del sur."[13]

En 1927, el Club de Artes y Oficios de Nueva Orleans montó una exposición de dibujos de arquitectura mexicana de la autoría de Spratling, que mostró el trabajo que Spratling realizó en México junto a sus bocetos arquitectónicos del barrio francés de Nueva Orleans. La reseña del periódico Times Picayune *sobre la exposición de Spratling expuso las fuertes similitudes visuales entre los bocetos de Spratling en México y en Nueva Orleans y señaló que las imágenes de México y de Luisiana se "mantienen fusionadas por una unidad considerable," y caracterizo a ambas imágenes como "escenas del sur," sin importar si se originaron en "los Estados Unidos o en su vecino país México."[14] Durante este período, la obra de artistas de Mexico y de*

work of artists like Boyd Cruise and Clarence Millet often reinforced this Southern connection. Both artists painted lush and romantic New Orleans courtyard and street scenes that portray New Orleans as an exotic locale more closely tied to South America and Europe than the United States. Boyd Cruise, for instance, made succulent still life paintings of both Mexican and Louisianan tropical fruits set amidst opulent colonial architecture and verdant landscape scenes that revel in both regions' exotic allure.

By 1928, *The Times-Picayune* had proclaimed Mexican artist Diego Rivera "the greatest painter on the North American continent," and announced a four-day-only show of Diego Rivera's watercolors and oils at the New Orleans Arts and Crafts Club that the paper advertised as Rivera's "first in New Orleans."[15] Rivera's work entranced Louisiana artists and critics, who appreciated its connection to Mexican art and culture as well as its powerful engagement with contemporary social and political issues. "Would that more art from below the Rio Grande might appear in New Orleans exhibitions," exclaimed one Louisiana journalist particularly enamored with the modern Mexican art increasingly on display in New Orleans.[16]

During this period, Louisianan artists like Spratling and Durieux became friends, colleagues and frequent collaborators with artists like Rivera, David Alfaro Siqueiros, and Emilio Amero, and began organizing joint exhibitions and in both New Orleans and in Mexico City. By the 1930s the New Orleans Arts and Crafts Club began organizing exhibitions that featured the work of Mexican and Louisianan artists side-by-side, showcasing the cultural connections between Mexico and Louisiana, and the artistic affinities between Mexican and Louisianan artists. In 1933, *The Times Picayune* announced an exhibition at the New Orleans Arts and Crafts Club of work by "leading Mexican artists" Diego Rivera, Rufino Tamayo, and Emilio Romero in which they juxtaposed work by these Mexican artists with pieces that Spratling and Durieux produced during past trips to Mexico. "William Spratling and Caroline Durieux," wrote New Orleans art critic Irene Cooper, "although not Mexican, are not misplaced in the group of Mexican artists. Both have lived in Mexico for several years and their work shows a strong Mexican trend."[17]

Luisiana como Boyd Cruise y Clarence Millet a menudo reforzaron esta conexión con el Sur. Ambos artistas pintaron escenas urbanas exuberantes y románticas de Nueva Orleans que la retratan como un lugar exótico más ligadas a América del Sur y Europa que a los Estados Unidos. Boyd Cruise, por ejemplo, hizo bodegones con exóticas frutas de México y Luisiana, situadas en medio de escenas opulentas de arquitectura colonial y paisajes que deleitan en el exótico encanto de ambas regiones.

Para 1928, el Times-Picayune había proclamado al artista mexicano Diego Rivera como "el pintor más grande en el continente de América del Norte" y anunció una exhibición de acuarelas y óleos de Diego Rivera en el Club de Artes y Oficio de Nueva Orleans que duraría sólo cuatro días, como la presentación de Rivera "por primera vez en Nueva Orleans."[15] El trabajo de Rivera asombró a artistas y críticos de Luisiana, los cuales apreciaron la conexión de su arte y de la cultura mexicana con la de ellos, así como su gran compromiso con las cuestiones sociales y políticas contemporáneas. "Ojalá que más arte proveniente del sur del Río Grande puede presentarse en exposiciones de Nueva Orleans", exclamó un periodista de Luisiana particularmente enamorado cada vez más del arte moderno mexicano expuesto en Nueva Orleans.[16] Durante este período, los artistas de Luisiana como Spratling y Durieux se hicieron amigos, colegas y colaboradores frecuentes de artistas como Rivera, David Alfaro Siqueiros, y Emilio Amero, y comenzaron a organizar exposiciones conjuntas, tanto en Nueva Orleans como en la Ciudad de México.

Por la década de 1930 el Club de Artes y Oficios de Nueva Orleans Artes comenzó a organizar exposiciones que mostraron el trabajo de artistas de México y de Luisiana conjuntamente, mostrando las conexiones culturales entre ambos lugares y las afinidades artísticas entre sus artistas. En 1933, el Times Picayune anunció una exposición en el Club de Artes y Oficios de Nueva Orleans con la obra de " los principales artistas mexicanos " Diego Rivera , Rufino Tamayo , y Emilio Romero en la que se mezclaron obra de estos artistas mexicanos con piezas que produjeron Spratling y Durieux durante viajes a México. "William Spratling y Caroline Durieux" escribió Irene Cooper, crítica de arte de Nueva Orleans "aunque no son mexicanos, no están fuera de lugar en el grupo de artistas mexicanos. Ambos han vivido en México desde hace varios años y su trabajo muestra.[17]

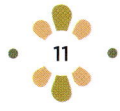

Louisiana printmaker Caroline Durieux, like Spratling, spent years living in Mexico and studying with Mexican artists like Rivera and Emilio Amero. She had a particularly close relationship with Rivera, who famously painted her portrait in 1929. Rivera's portrait of Durieux captured the vibrant artistic and cultural exchange between Mexican and Louisianan artists of this period, and was exhibited multiple times both in Mexico and New Orleans. Hinting at the strength of Durieux's connection to Mexican artists like Rivera and his wife, Frida Kahlo, the New Orleans artist Olive Leonhardt wrote of the portrait's frequent appearance at the Belles Artes in Mexico City, where it was often shown alongside Frida Kahlo's self-portrait *Me and My Parrots.* In addition to the frequent joint appearances of these paired portraits in Mexico, they were also shown side-by-side in New Orleans in February of 1942, when the Arts and Crafts Club mounted a show of Mexican art that included Rivera's portrait of Durieux alongside some ribald political prints by Emilio Amero. [18]

Durieux moved to Mexico in 1926 and, like Spratling, spent years living and working in the country. She worked closely with Mexican artists like Rivera and Amero to hone her printmaking technique and the satirical sensibilities she began developing in her work in New Orleans in the early 1920s. In the parodic and politically charged work of these post-Revolutionary Mexican artists, Durieux found a match for her sardonic wit and strong satirical sensibilities, as well as her interest in experimental printmaking techniques. While in Mexico, Durieux worked closely with Amero, who had established a lithography studio where he instructed young artists like Durieux in printmaking techniques. Her satirical Mexican prints of the period such as *Dressmaking* reflect the modern, graphic style of Amero's prints like *Where? Donde?,* as well as his tendency to poke fun at Mexico's political elite. [19]

In 1929, the same year as he painted her portrait, Diego Rivera wrote an impassioned review of Durieux's work in *Mexican Folkways* that high-lighted her strong connection to Mexico and "clear eye" for political satire:

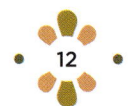

La grabadora de Luisiana Caroline Durieux, como Spratling, pasó años viviendo en México y estudió con artistas mexicanos como Diego Rivera y Emilio Amero. Ella tenía una relación particularmente estrecha con Rivera, quien pintó su famoso retrato en 1929. una fuerte tendencia mexicana". El retrato que Rivera hiciera de Durieux, capturó el vibrante intercambio artístico y cultural entre artistas mexicanos y de Luisiana de este período y participo en exhibiciones en varias ocasiones en México y Nueva Orleans. Haciendo alusión a la fuerte conexión de Durieux con artistas mexicanos como Rivera y su esposa, Frida Kahlo, la artista de Nueva Orleans Olive Leonhardt escribió sobre la frecuente aparición del retrato en el Palacio de Bellas Artes en la Ciudad de México, donde se mostraba a menudo junto con el autorretrato de Frida Kahlo "Yo y mis loros." Además de las apariciones frecuentes de estos retratos en México, también se mostraron conjuntamente en Nueva Orleans en febrero de 1942, cuando el Club de las Artes y Oficios montó un exposición de arte mexicano que incluyó el retrato pintado por Rivera de Durieux junto algunas impresiones políticas de Emilio Amero. [18]

Durieux se trasladó a México en 1926 y al igual que Spratling, pasó años viviendo y trabajando en el país. Ella trabajó en estrecha colaboración con los artistas mexicanos, Rivera y Amero, para perfeccionar su técnica de grabado, así como su sensibilidad satírica que comenzó a desarrollar en su trabajo realizado en Nueva Orleans a principios del 1920. En la obra paródica y políticamente saturada de estos artistas post revolucionarios mexicanos, Durieux se encontró su ingenio sarcástico y su fuerte sensibilidad satírica, así como su interés por las técnicas de grabado experimentales. Durante su estancia en México, Durieux trabajó estrechamente con Amero, que había establecido un estudio de litografía donde instruía a jóvenes artistas como Durieux en técnicas de grabado. Sus grabados satíricos mexicanos de la época, tales como "Corte y confección" reflejan el estilo moderno de los grabados de Amero, tales como "Where? ¿Dónde?", así como su tendencia a burlarse de la élite política de México. [19]

En 1929, el mismo año en que Diego Rivera pintó su retrato, escribió una crítica apasionada de la obra de Durieux en Mexican Folkways, donde destacó su fuerte conexión con México y sus "ojos claros" para la sátira política:

Since she has lived among us, she has developed a close spiritual rapport with the country and simultaneously there has grown in her a painter's mature power of expression. Not only does her painting show her love of nature, exalting the grandeur of the mountains, the beauty of the peasants, and the orderly freedom of our architecture, but she has also seen our mongrel, perverted, and deformed bourgeoisie, with the clear eye of a Mexican mountaineer, and yet with all of the urbanity, the culture, and the occidental sophistication which are Caroline's.[20]

In 1934, Durieux organized a major exhibition of over forty prints at the Galería Central in Mexico City that incorporated her work from Mexico and her work from New Orleans. During her time in Mexico, Durieux created a series of drawings, prints, and paintings like *Priests* that poked fun at the pretensions of upper-crust politicians, society ladies, and priests, and reflected much the same spirit she would bring to later prints of similar subject matter in New Orleans such as *In the French Quarter, New Orleans.* A Mexican writer for *El Excelsior* wrote that the exhibition reflected Durieux's

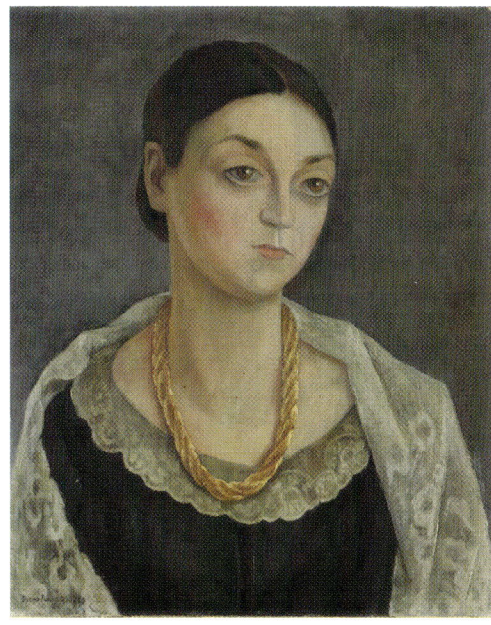

Puesto que ella ha vivido entre nosotros, ella ha desarrollado una relación espiritual estrecha con el país y al mismo tiempo ha crecido en su poder de expresión, madurando como pintora. No sólo su pintura muestra su amor por la naturaleza, la cual exalta la grandeza de las montañas, la belleza de los campesinos y la libertad ordenada de nuestra arquitectura, pero también ha visto nuestra pervertida y deformada burguesía, con el ojo claro de una alpinista mexicana, y sin embargo, con toda la urbanidad, la cultura y la sofisticación occidental que son atributos de Caroline.[20]

En 1934, Durieux organizó una gran exposición de más de cuarenta grabados en la Galería Central de la Ciudad de México, la cual incorporó su trabajo de México y su trabajo de Nueva Orleans. Durante su estancia en México, Durieux creó una serie de dibujos, grabados y pinturas tipo Sacerdotes, *en donde se burló de las pretensiones de los políticos de las altas esferas, de las damas de la sociedad y de los clérigos, reflejando así el mismo espíritu en sus trabajos posteriores, de temas similares creados* En el Barrio francés de Nueva Orleans. *Un escritor mexicano del periódico* El Excélsior *escribió que la exposición de Durieux, reflejaba "una visión implacable de la escena social aquí" y mostró la "nitidez de sus*

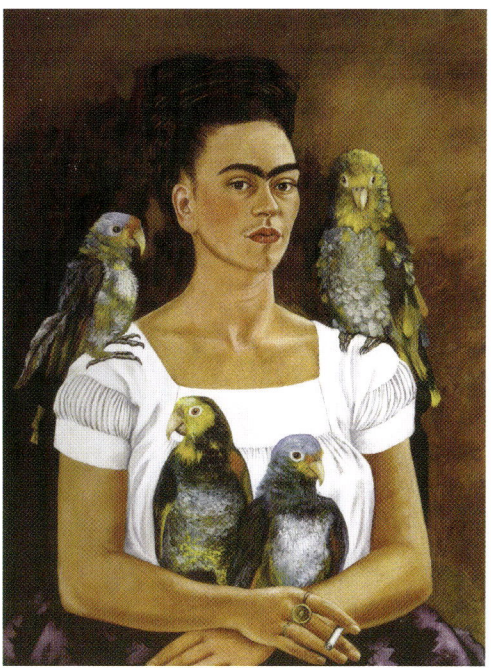

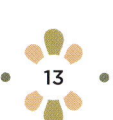

"relentless insight on the social scene here" and showcased the "sharpness of her conclusions" about contemporary society.[21] Rivera wrote that Durieux's work was "at once politely cruel and charmingly venomous."[22] He saw in her satirical prints a spirit of "caustic irony" that matched his own critiques of Mexico's upper class.[23] *The Times-Picayune* likewise lauded her artful satire, and made particular note of her strong connection to Mexico. "Sometimes brutal but always clever in her portrayal of human nature," the article wrote, "Caroline Durieux, formerly of New Orleans and now of Taxco, Mexico, has gained international recognition in the artistic world with almost phenomenal swiftness through her social satires and symbolic stylizations."[24]

Durieux, who taught at Louisiana State University from 1943 to 1964, came from a well-heeled family in New Orleans and was part of a group of young New Orleans artists and writers from the 1920s who sought

conclusiones" sobre la sociedad contemporánea.[21] Rivera escribió que el trabajo de Durieux fue "a la vez educadamente cruel y encantadoramente venenoso."[22] Él vio en sus grabados satíricos un espíritu de "ironía cáustica" que hacía juego con sus propias críticas de la clase alta de México.[23] El Times-Picayune igualmente elogió su sátira ingeniosa, e hizo especial nota de su fuerte conexión con México. "A veces brutal, pero siempre inteligente en su interpretación de la naturaleza humana", escribió el artículo, "Caroline Durieux, residente anteriormente de Nueva Orleans y ahora de Taxco, México, ha ganado el reconocimiento internacional en el mundo artístico con una rapidez casi fenomenal a través de sus sátiras sociales y estilizaciones simbólicas".[24]

Durieux provenía de una familia adinerada, en Nueva Orleans, y fue parte de un grupo de jóvenes artistas y escritores de los años 1920 Nueva Orleans, que se proponía introducir una nueva conciencia política en el

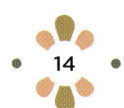

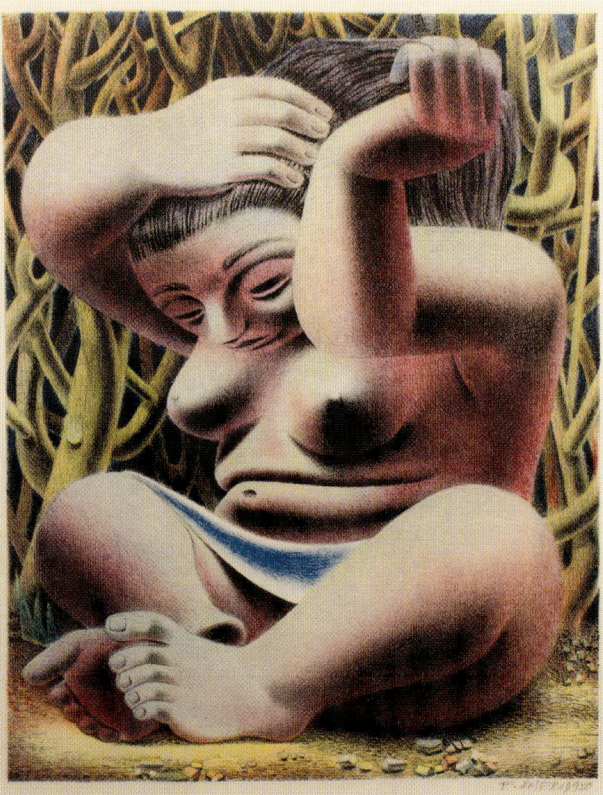

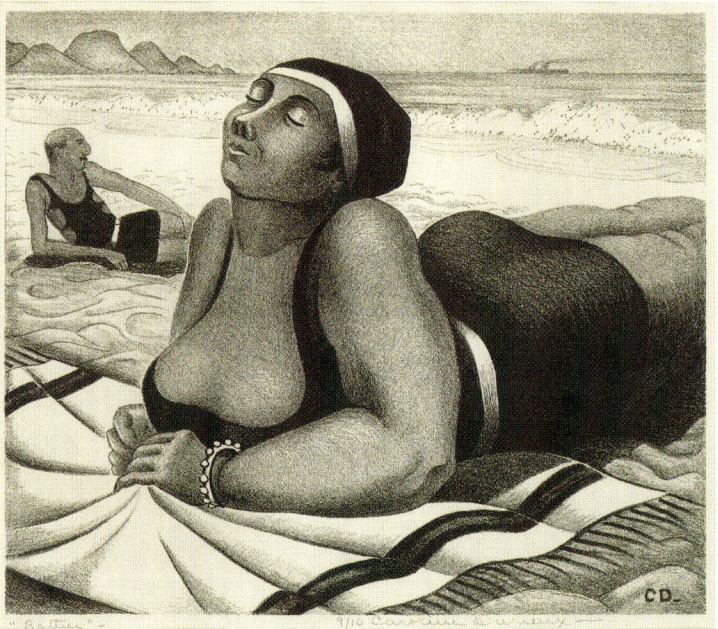

Left:
EMILIO AMERO
Girl Combing Her Hair/Muchacha Peinandose, 1950
Color lithographic ink on warm white rag paper
Meadows Museum of Art
Stein Collection of Don Brown Works

Above:
CAROLINE WOGAN DURIEUX
Bather, 1932
Lithograph on paper
LSU Museum of Art, 68.9.4
Gift of the Artist

to introduce a new political consciousness into Louisiana art and often critiqued the conservatism of upper-crust New Orleans society. This group included artists like Spratling, Blom, and Durieux's friend Olive Leonhardt, among others. Many of these artists went on to spend considerable time living and working in Mexico in the 1930s. Durieux shared a studio with Leonhardt in the early 1920s, and Leonhardt joined Durieux in Mexico in the 1930s, lured there in part by Durieux's successful collaborations with Mexican printmakers and political cartoonists. From the early 1920s, the women had shared a similar seriousness of purpose as artists, with one New Orleans newspaper writing with some astonishment in a 1921 review of an exhibition the two women co-hosted in their art studio, "these girls have done more than play at being artists."[25]

Like Durieux, Leonhardt's time in Mexico proved formative for her artistic development, and she incorporated many of the artistic lessons

arte Luisiana, a menudo criticando el conservadurismo de la clase alta de la sociedad de Nueva Orleans. Este grupo incluía a artistas como Spratling, Blom y el amigo de Durieux, Olive Leonhardt , entre otros. Muchos de estos artistas pasaron un tiempo considerable viviendo y trabajando en México en la década de 1930. Durieux compartió un estudio con Leonhardt a principios de 1920 en Nueva Orleans y se reunió con Durieux en México en la década de 1930, atraída en parte por las colaboraciones exitosas de Durieux con grabadores mexicanos y caricaturistas políticos. Desde la década de 1920, las mujeres habían compartido un similar propósito como artistas, un periódico de Nueva Orleans escribió con cierto asombro en una revisión de la exposición que las dos mujeres organizaron en1921 en su estudio de arte, "estas chicas han hecho más que solo jugar a ser artistas."[25]

Al igual que Durieux, el tiempo de Leonhardt en México demostró ser un periodo formativo para su desarrollo artístico e incorporó muchas de

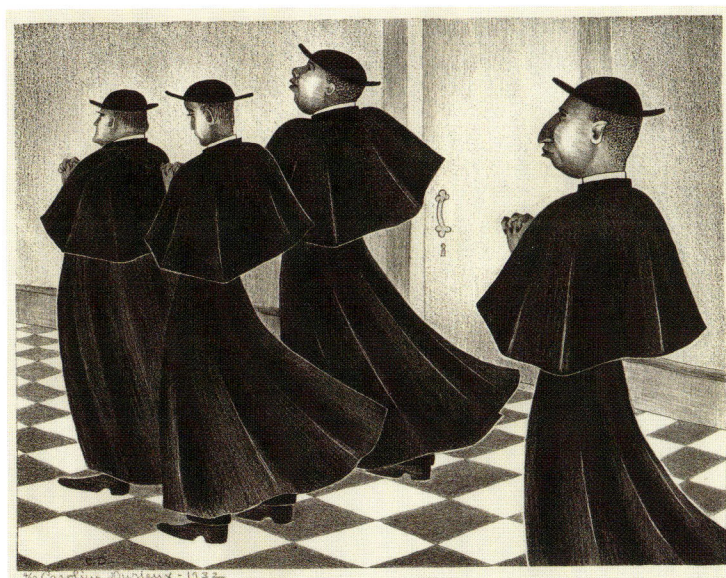

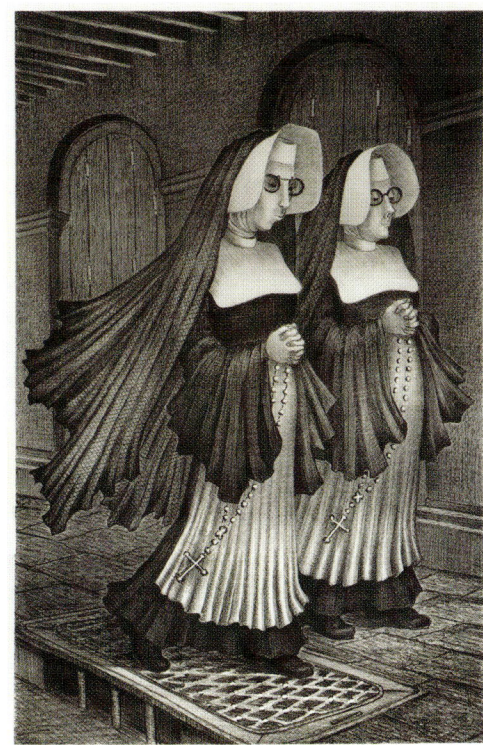

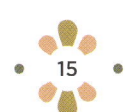

Above:
CAROLINE WOGAN DURIEUX
Priests, 1932
Lithograph on paper
LSU Museum of Art, 68.9.1
Gift of the Artist

Right:
CAROLINE WOGAN DURIEUX
In the French Quarter, New Orleans, 1945
Black lithograph on paper
LSU Museum of Art,68.9.29
Gift of the Artist

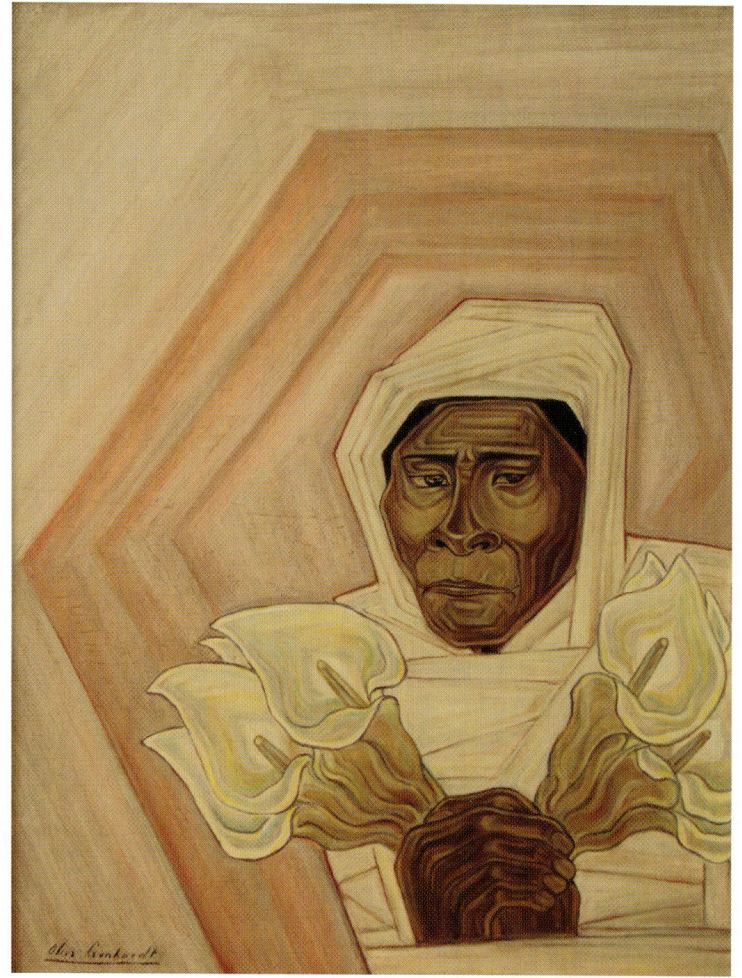

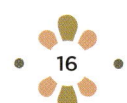

she learned in Mexico into her work in New Orleans. While in Mexico, Leonhardt developed a striking compositional style in paintings like *Blessed Virgin Returns to the Fiesta* that she exported directly into paintings of New Orleans subject matter like *Convent of the Holy Family, New Orleans.* In a 1931 interview with New Orleans journalist Daisy Weinberg, Leonhardt noted the strong influence that politically minded artists like Diego Rivera were having on Louisiana artists living and working in Mexico. Leonhardt saw the more politically minded art she encountered in Mexico as a necessary response to a time of great social and political upheaval, and a strong positive sign for painting's progress. "Our entire religious, social, and economic upheaval—this sounds pedantic but it's true—is going to leave us better painters," said Leonhardt. "We are coming to times of more sincerity."[26]

Leonhardt struck a much more cautious note than many of her contemporaries about the art being created by New Orleans artists living and working in Mexico. Unlike Spratling and Durieux, Leonhardt's primary focus during her time in Mexico was to study styles and

las lecciones artísticas que aprendió en México en su trabajo en Nueva Orleans. Mientras que en México, Leonhardt desarrolló un estilo de composición llamativa en pinturas como "Devoluciones Santísima Virgen a la Fiesta" que exportó directamente en pinturas sobre Nueva Orleans con motivos como el "Convento de la Sagrada Familia en Nueva Orleans." En una entrevista de 1931 con la periodista de New Orleans, Daisy Weinberg, Leonhardt señaló la fuerte influencia que artistas políticamente afines a Diego Rivera tenían en artistas de Luisiana que estaban viviendo y trabajando en México. Leonhardt vio el arte politizado que encontró en México, como una respuesta necesaria a una época de gran agitación social y política, siendo una señal fuerte y positiva para el progreso de la pintura. "Toda nuestra conmoción religiosa, social y económica suena pedante, pero en verdad nos va a hacer mejores pintores", dijo Leonhardt. "Estamos llegando a los momentos de mayor sinceridad."[26]

Leonhardt dio una pauta mucho más moderada que muchos de sus contemporáneos, con respecto al arte creado por artistas de Nueva Orleans que estaban viviendo y trabajando en México. A diferencia de Spratling y Durieux, el enfoque principal de Leonhardt durante su

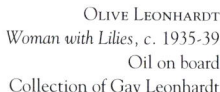

OLIVE LEONHARDT
Woman with Lilies, c. 1935-39
Oil on board
Collection of Gay Leonhardt

forms she could export into more local subject matter, and particularly representations of life in the American South. In an interview entitled *She Tells New Orleans Painters to Paint New Orleans Things*, Leonhardt voiced her concerns about the benefits of cross-cultural collaboration, which, to her mind, had New Orleans artists painting "picturesque" Mexican scenes rather than focusing their attention on people and places closer to home. "Isn't it natural," she said "that growing up in Jackson, Mississippi, going to school at Newcomb and living in New Orleans for years, I should get the feeling of local people and places? For myself, I think I do better sketching a Mississippi boy, impudent and shy, at the same time, rather than trying to do picturesque Mexicans [or] tropical foliage."[27]

Leonhardt encouraged Louisianans to focus in on more local subject matter so that they might delve more deeply into aspects of life in New Orleans often lost in more "picturesque" views of these places. During this period, Louisiana artists like Boyd Cruise and Morris Henry Hobbs often offered parallel visions of Mexico and Louisiana as picturesque

estancia en México fue el estudio de estilos y formas que podía expresar con temas más comunes, que representaran de la vida cotidiana de Sudamérica. En una entrevista titulada "Ella le dice a los pintores de Nueva Orleans pintar acerca de Nueva Orleans", Leonhardt expresó sus preocupaciones acerca de los beneficios de la colaboración intercultural, que, en su opinión, mantuvo a artistas de Nueva Orleans produciendo "pintorescas" escenas mexicanas en lugar de centrar su atención en personas y lugares más cercanos a casa". "¿Debe ser natural", dijo "que al habiendo crecido en Jackson, Mississippi, haber atendido la escuela en Newcomb y haber viviendo en Nueva Orleans durante años, deba tener sensibilidad por la gente local y los lugares locales? En cuanto a mí, creo que me es mejor dibujar un niño de Mississippi, insolente y tímido, en lugar de tratar de dibujar niños mexicanos, o paisajes tropicales".[27]

Leonhardt alentó a artistas de Luisiana a centrarse en temas más locales para que pudieran profundizar en aspectos de la vida de Nueva Orleans, y así no perderse dentro de más "pintorescos" temas de otros lugares. Durante este período, los artistas de Luisiana como Boyd Cruise y Morris Henry Hobbs a menudo ofrecían visiones paralelas entre México y

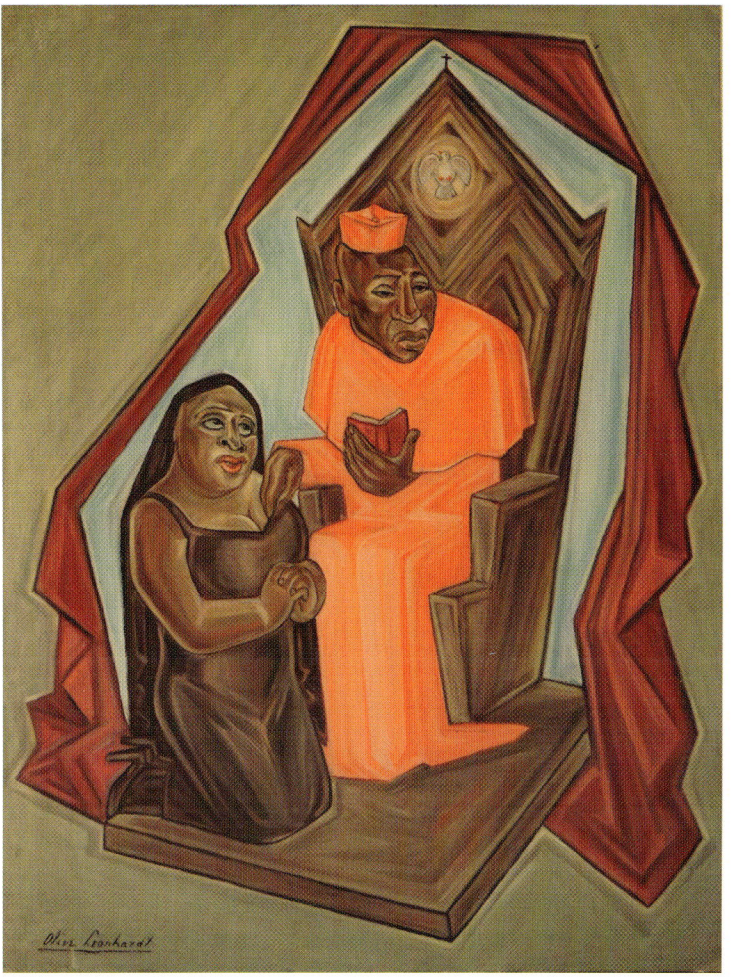

Olive Leonhardt
Convent of the Holy Family, New Orleans, c. 1935-39
Oil on board
Collection of Gay Leonhardt

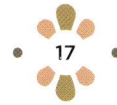

places untouched by time and at a remove from contemporary social and political issues. Hobbs' etchings of Mexico, like his etchings of New Orleans, portrayed both places more as exotic tourist destinations than living, breathing contemporary cities—places of great beauty, to be sure, but places unencumbered by the political questions that enlivened the work of artists like Spratling and Durieux, and many of the Mexican artists they worked alongside.[28] However, for most Louisiana artists, it was precisely the fusion of formal beauty and conceptual sophistication that drew them to Mexican art, which, as Frances Toor wrote, was often seen by Americans as "food for the intellect because of subject matter [and] for the spirit because of form and color."[29]

If artists like Leonhardt encouraged Louisianans to look local, other artists like Elizabeth Catlett saw global connections between Mexico and the American South. African-American sculptor and printmaker Elizabeth Catlett taught at Dillard University in New Orleans in 1940s, and was made an honorary citizen of the city for her influential sculptures and prints depicting African-American life in the American South. Catlett

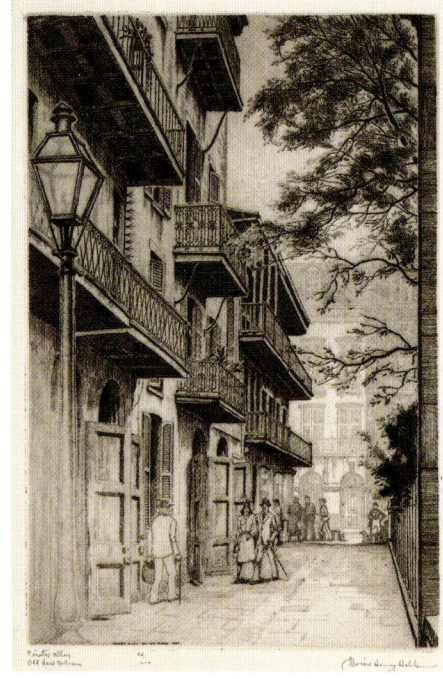

MORRIS HENRY HOBBS
Pirates Alley, Old New Orleans, 1943
Etching on paper
Private Collection
Photo © David Humphreys, 2015

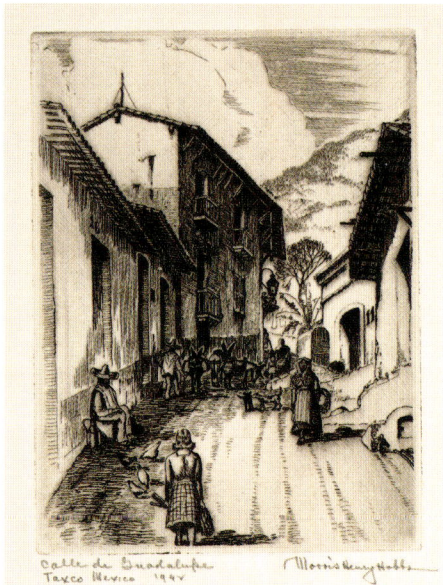

Morris Henry Hobbs
Calle de Guadalupe, Taxco, Mexico, 1942
Etching on paper
LSU Museum of Art, MOA 10.205.23
Gift of Dr. A. Brooks Cronan, Jr. and Diana Cronan
Photo © David Humphreys, 2015

Luisiana, como lugares pintorescos indemnes por el tiempo y la distancia de los problemas sociales y políticos contemporáneos. Los aguafuertes de Hobbs acerca de México, al igual que sus aguafuertes de Nueva Orleans, retrataron los dos lugares más como destinos turísticos exóticos que como ciudades contemporáneos y lugares de gran belleza, pero sin duda sin el molestia de las cuestiones políticas que extasiaron la obra de artistas como Spratling y Durieux, así como el de muchos de los artistas mexicanos que trabajaron junto con ellos.[28] Sin embargo, para la mayoría de los artistas de Luisiana, fue precisamente la fusión de la belleza formal y la sofisticación conceptual lo que los atrajo del arte mexicano, que, como escribió Frances Toor, se contempla a menudo por los estadounidenses como "alimento para el intelecto, debido a sus temas, y para el espíritu por su forma y color".[29]

Si artistas como Leonhardt animaban a artistas de Luisiana a buscar temas locales, otros artistas como Elizabeth Catlett vieron conexiones globales entre México y el sur de Estados Unidos. Escultora y grabadora afroamericana, Elizabeth Catlett enseñó en la Universidad de Dillard en Nueva Orleans en 1940 y fue nombrada ciudadana honoraria de la ciudad

received an art fellowship to study in Mexico in 1946 and remained in the country for the rest of her life, becoming an influential teacher at the famed Mexico City printmaking collective Taller de Gráphica Popular. After an arrest at a Mexico City political protest put her under surveillance by the United States Embassy, she was barred from re-entering the United States and, in 1962, renounced her United States citizenship to become an official Mexican citizen.

While living in Mexico, Catlett created her renowned *The Negro Woman* series, which chronicles the experiences of African-American women in the United States in 15 prints that portray African-American artists, writers, and activists like Sojourner Truth alongside images of slavery and oppression. Creating this series about African-American experience in the United States while living and working in Mexico, Catlett saw clear corollaries between political conditions in Mexico and the lives of African-American people in the United States, viewing both countries as participating in a shared struggle for liberation and freedom. "I was born in the United States and have lived in Mexico since 1946," Catlett wrote. "I believe all these states of being have influenced my work and made it what you see today. I am inspired by black people and Mexican people, my two peoples. My art speaks for both my peoples." In Mexico, Catlett wrote, she "learned how you use your art for the service of people, struggling people, to whom only realism is meaningful."[30]

Artists Conrad Albrizio, Enrique Alferez, and Edward Millman all created large-scale public art projects in Louisiana inspired, in part, by their time studying with Diego Rivera and other Mexican muralists in Mexico. All three artists worked in Louisiana as part of the Works Progress Administration, which sponsored Albrizio's murals and mosaics, Alferez's sculptures and friezes, and Millman's series of pastels and watercolors documenting life on Louisiana's bayous in the 1940s. The Mexican-born sculptor Enrique Alferez made New Orleans his home in 1929, and his dynamic public sculptures throughout New Orleans reflect his belief in public art's ability to advance the cause of the common man.[31] Albrizio's murals throughout Baton Rouge and on Louisiana State University's campus were likewise inspired by Mexican mural traditions, and in 1949 Millman mounted an exhibition of his pastels and watercolors at LSU that reflected the clear influence of Rivera's work.

por logros con sus esculturas y grabados de la vida afroamericana en el Sur. Catlett recibió una beca para estudiar arte en México en 1946 y permaneció en el país durante el resto de su vida, convirtiéndose en una influyente profesora en el famoso Taller de Gráfica Colectiva Popular de la Ciudad de México. Después de un arresto en una protesta política en la Ciudad de México, la Embajada de Estados Unidos la puso bajo la vigilancia y se le prohibió volver a entrar en los Estados Unidos. En 1962 renunció a su ciudadanía norteamericana para convertirse oficialmente en una ciudadana mexicana.

Mientras vivía en México, Catlett creó su famosa serie "La Mujer Negra", que narra las experiencias de las mujeres afroamericanas en los Estados Unidos en 15 grabados, que retratan a los artistas afroamericanos, escritores y activistas como Sojourner Truth, junto a imágenes de la esclavitud y la opresión. La creación de esta serie sobre la experiencia afroamericana en los Estados Unidos, mientras vivía y trabajaba en México, dio a Catlett la visión de claras similitudes entre las condiciones políticas en México y la vida de los afroamericanos en los Estados Unidos, viendo que ambos países participaban en la misma lucha por la liberación y la libertad. "Yo nací en los Estados Unidos y he vivido en México desde 1946," escribió Catlett. "Creo que todas estas formas de bienestar han influido en mi trabajo y lo ha hecho lo que se ve hoy en día. Me inspiro en los negros y los mexicanos, mis dos pueblos. Mi arte habla por mis dos pueblos." En México, Catlett escribió que ella "aprendió cómo utilizar su arte al servicio de la gente, a la gente que lucha, a la que sólo el realismo es significativo".[30]

Los artistas Conrad Albrizio, Enrique Alférez y Edward Millman crearon proyectos de arte público a gran escala en Luisiana, inspirados en parte, por el tiempo que estudiaron con Diego Rivera y otros muralistas mexicanos en México. Los tres artistas trabajaron en Luisiana como parte del Works Progress Administration, que patrocinó murales y mosaicos de Albrizio, esculturas y frisos de Alférez y series de pasteles y acuarelas de Millman, que documentan la vida en los pantanos de Luisiana en la década de 1940. El escultor nacido en México, Enrique Alférez hizo Nueva Orleans su casa en 1929 y sus esculturas de gran dinamismo expuestas en de Nueva Orleans reflejan su creencia en la capacidad del arte público para promover la causa del hombre común.[31]

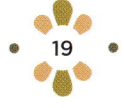

Millman travelled to Mexico to study with Rivera in 1935, and his exhibition at LSU mined his earlier work in Mexico to highlight issues of racism and social injustice in Louisiana and support the cause of working class people living on Louisiana's bayous.

In the early 1930s, the strength of the artistic interaction between Mexico and Louisiana caused a writer for *The Times-Picayune* to characterize Louisianan art as having a "distinct Mexican tinge" that influenced

Los murales de Albrizio en todo Baton Rouge y en el campus de la Universidad Estatal de Luisiana (LSU) fueron igualmente inspirados en las tradiciones muralistas mexicanas. En 1949 Millman montó una exposición de sus pasteles y acuarelas en LSU que reflejaban la clara influencia de la obra de Rivera.

Millman viajó a México para estudiar con Rivera en 1935 y su exposición en LSU mostro su anterior trabajo en México como forma de resaltar los problemas del racismo y la injusticia social en Luisiana y así apoyar la causa de la gente de clase trabajadora que vivía en los pantanos de Luisiana.

A principios de 1930, la fuerza de la interacción artística entre México y Luisiana influyo en un escritor del El Times–Picayune, *en caracterizar el arte de Luisiana de tener un " tinte mexicano muy característico" en*

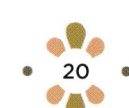

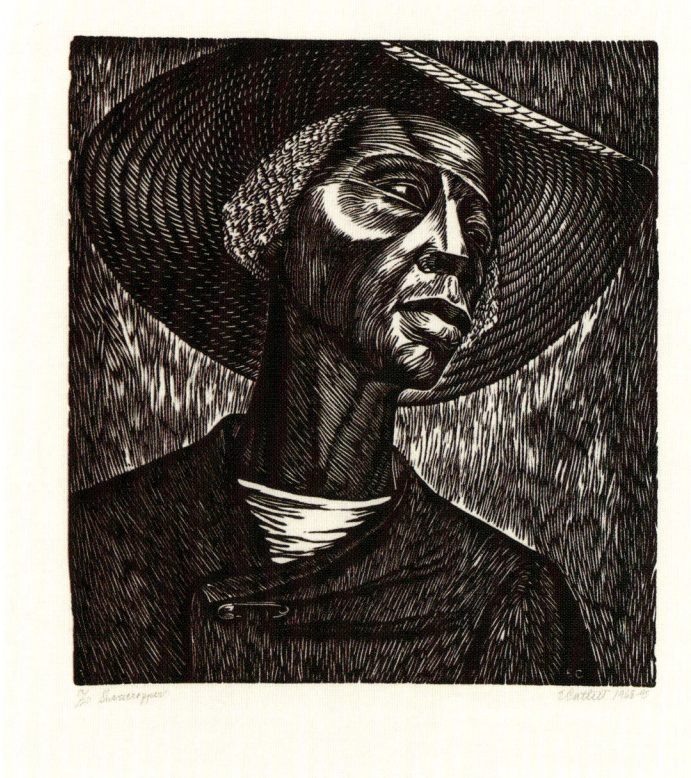
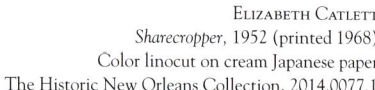

ELIZABETH CATLETT
Sharecropper, 1952 (printed 1968)
Color linocut on cream Japanese paper
The Historic New Orleans Collection, 2014.0077.1

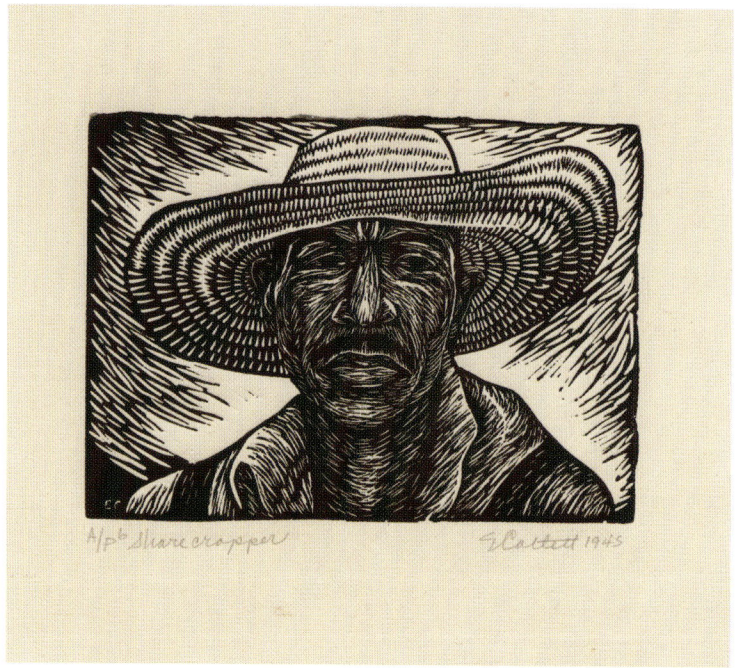

ELIZABETH CATLETT
[Male] Sharecropper, 1945
Woodcut
The Historic New Orleans Collection, 2014.0077.3

Louisiana art on the level of form and composition, and also helped inspire a stronger level of political engagement on the part of artists working in New Orleans.[32] The close friendships between Mexican and Louisiana artists of the 1920s through 1950s resulted in a decades-long dialogue between Mexican and Louisianan artists which critically shaped the art of both countries, and created cultural and artistic affinities between the two regions that continue to connect Louisiana and Mexico today.

comparación con el arte de artistas de color de Luisiana con respecto a la forma y la composición y también ayudó a inspirar a mostrar un mayor nivel de compromiso político a los artistas que trabajan en Nueva Orleans.[32] La estrecha amistad entre artistas mexicanos y de Luisiana de la década de 1920 a hasta 1950 dio lugar a un diálogo entre artistas mexicanos y Luisiana, que duró décadas, que de forma crítica marcó el arte de ambos países, creando así afinidades culturales y artísticas entre las dos regiones, mismas que continúan enlazando a Luisiana y a México hoy en día.

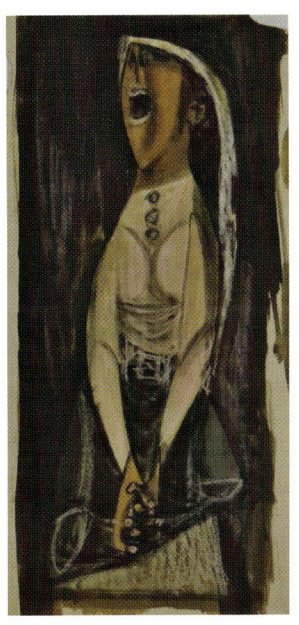

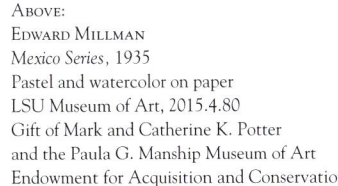

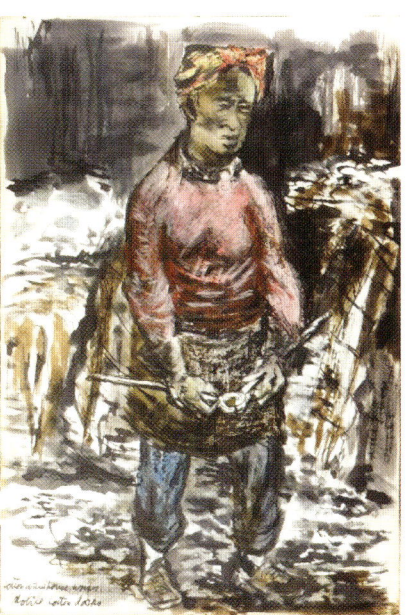

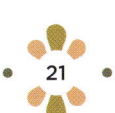

Above:
Edward Millman
Mexico Series, 1935
Pastel and watercolor on paper
LSU Museum of Art, 2015.4.80
Gift of Mark and Catherine K. Potter
and the Paula G. Manship Museum of Art
Endowment for Acquisition and Conservation

Right:
Edward Millman
Bayou Nutria Series, 1939
LSU Museum of Art
Gift of Mark and Catherine K. Potter
and the Paula G. Manship Museum of Art
Endowment for Acquisition and Conservation

Elizabeth Catlett
Young Mexican Girl/Niña, 1945-1947
Color serigraph
The Historic New Orleans Collection, 2014.0077.6

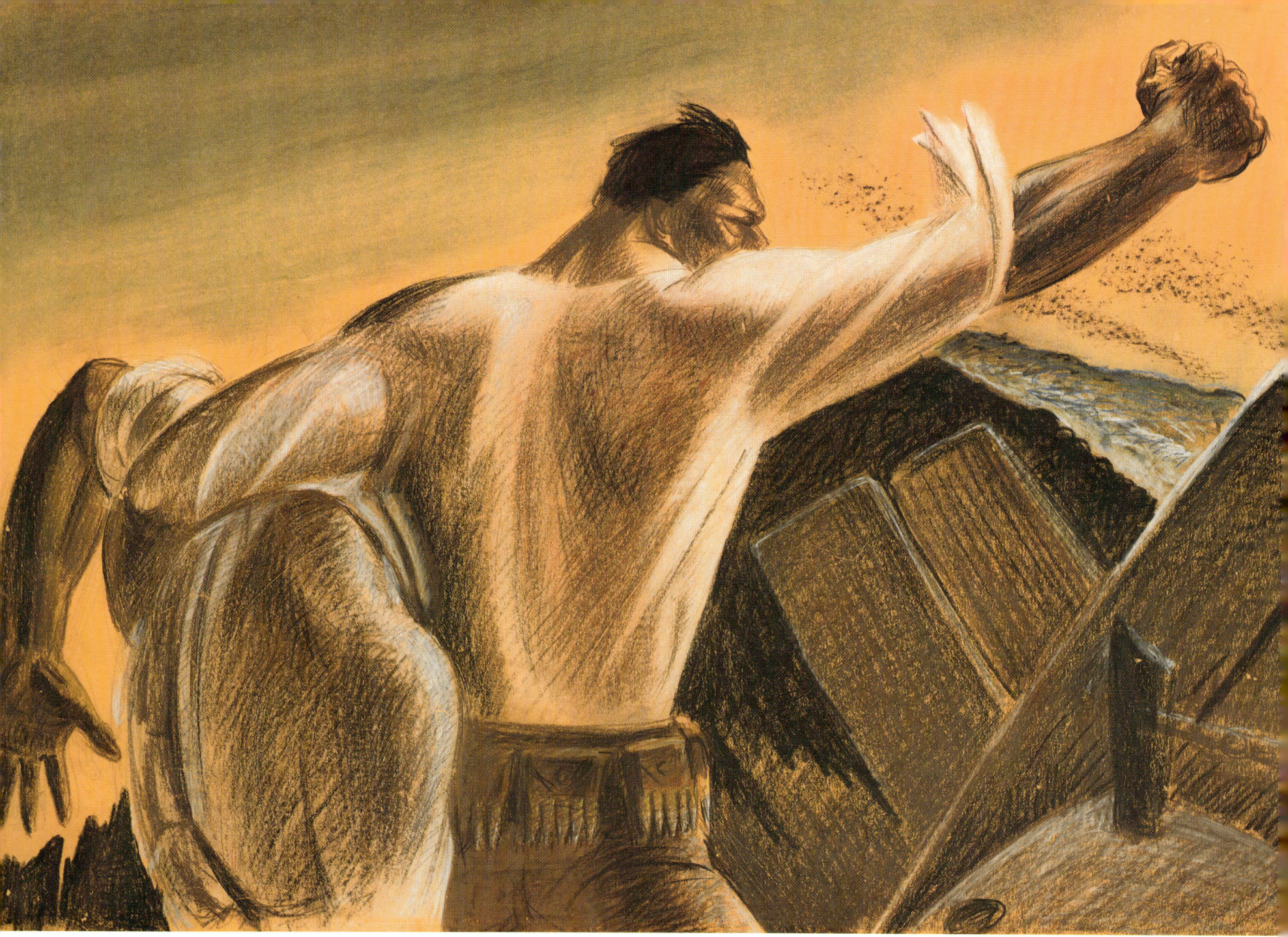

Enrique Alferez
Drawing of a Man, 1940
Crayon on orange paper
The Historic New Orleans Collection, 1968.12.1
Gift of Mr. Albert L. Lieutaud

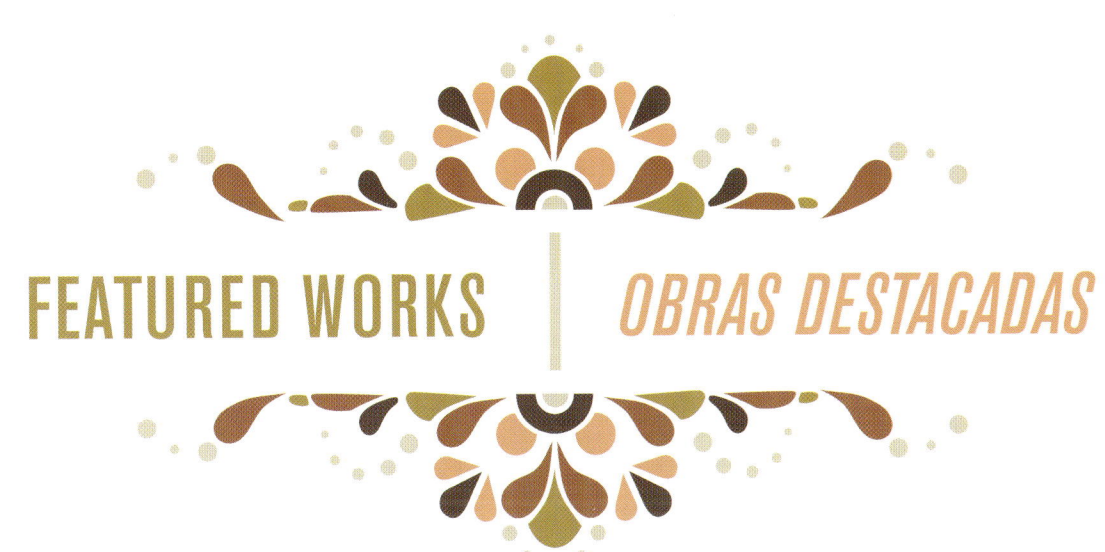

FEATURED WORKS | OBRAS DESTACADAS

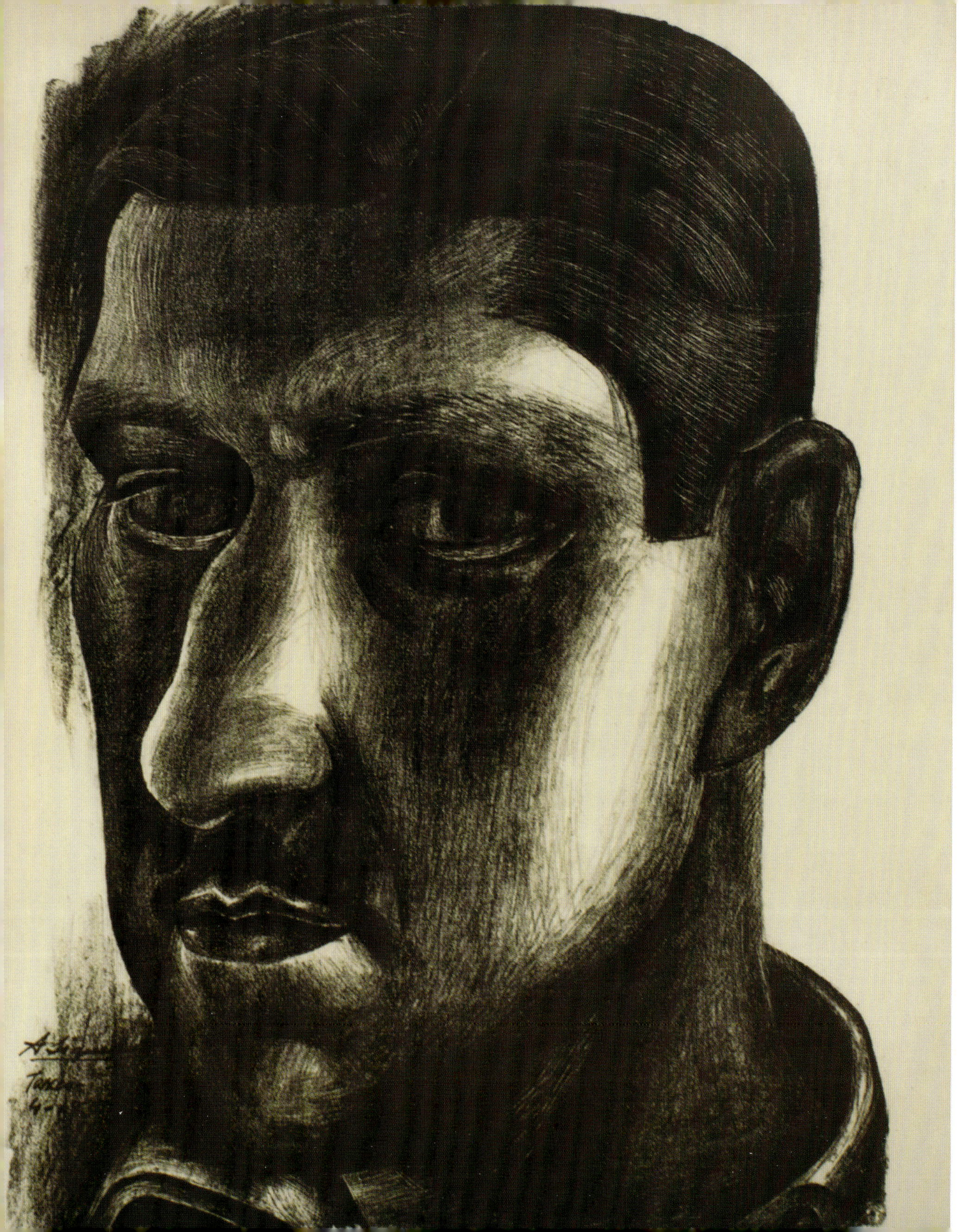

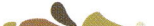

DAVID ALFARO SIQUEIROS
Spratling, u.d.
Lithograph on paper
The Latin American Library, Tulane University
Spratling-Taxco Collection

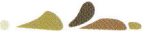

While in Mexico, Spratling developed a close relationship with the Mexican muralist and printmaker David Alfaro Siqueiros. The two artists had a deep respect for each other's work and often collaborated on joint projects, such as this portrait Siqueiros made of Spratling. In a 1931 essay about Siqueiros, Spratling described Siqueiros as a "profoundly significant figure in modorn Mexican painting," and praised him for "a simplicity and power in his use of form and color that few painters today may scarcely be said to approach."

WILLIAM SPRATLING
Maguey, u.d.
Ink and charcoal on white paper
The Latin American Library, Tulane University
Spratling-Taxco Collection

In 1932, Spratling published an illustrated travelogue about his time in Mexico entitled *Little Mexico.* This drawing of the town of Acuitlapan comes from that book, which Spratling filled with illustrations of contemporary Mexican scenes whose forms recall the ancient Pre-Columbian clay seal stamp imprints he studied while in Mexico. Spratling's work in Mexico often sought to create visual ties between Mexico's past art and its present-day landscapes and peoples, linking ancient and modern artistic forms.

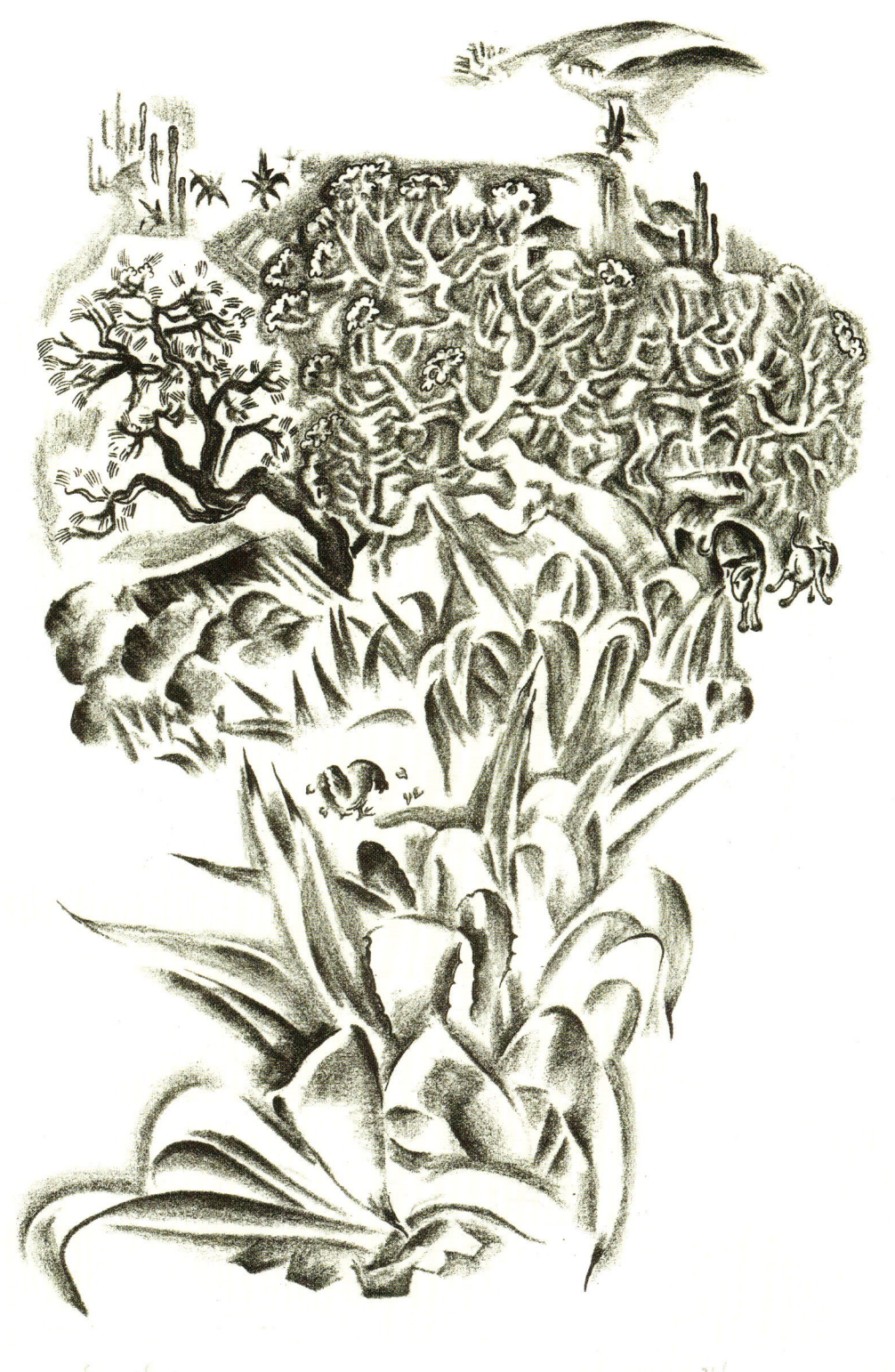

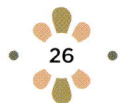

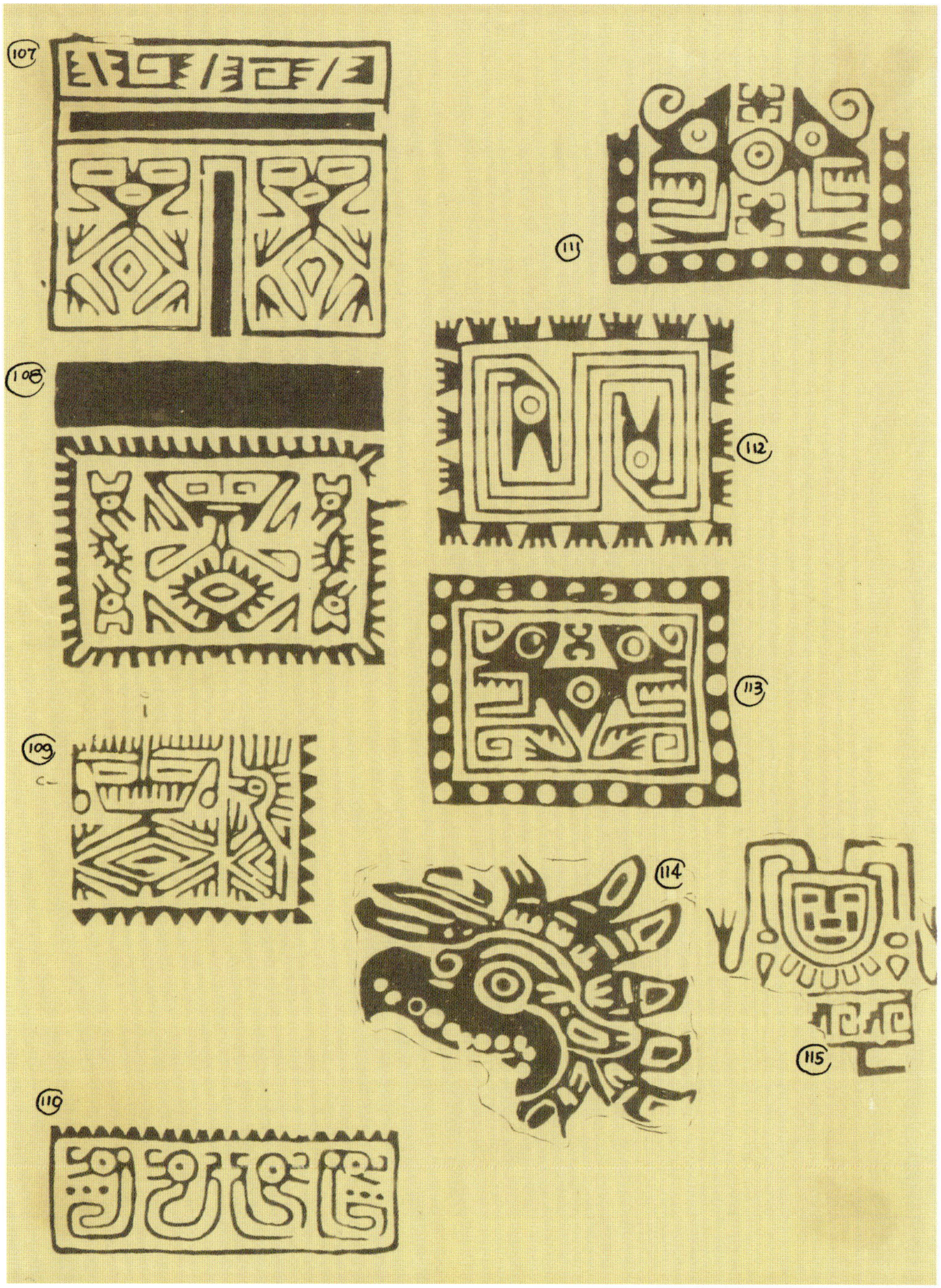

WILLIAM SPRATLING
Pre-Columbian Clay Seal Stamp Imprints 107-115, u.d.
Photostatic copy on paper
The Latin American Library, Tulane University
Spratling-Taxco Collection

While in Mexico, Spratling's close friendship with the archaeologist Frans Blom resulted in considerable exposure to ancient Pre-Columbian and Mesoamerican art. These Pre-Columbian clay seal stamp imprints would have been used to stamp patterns on clay. The patterns and forms of Pre-Columbian art hugely influenced not just Spratling's work in jewelry design, but also his overall design aesthetic in his furniture, decorative art objects, and architectural drawings.

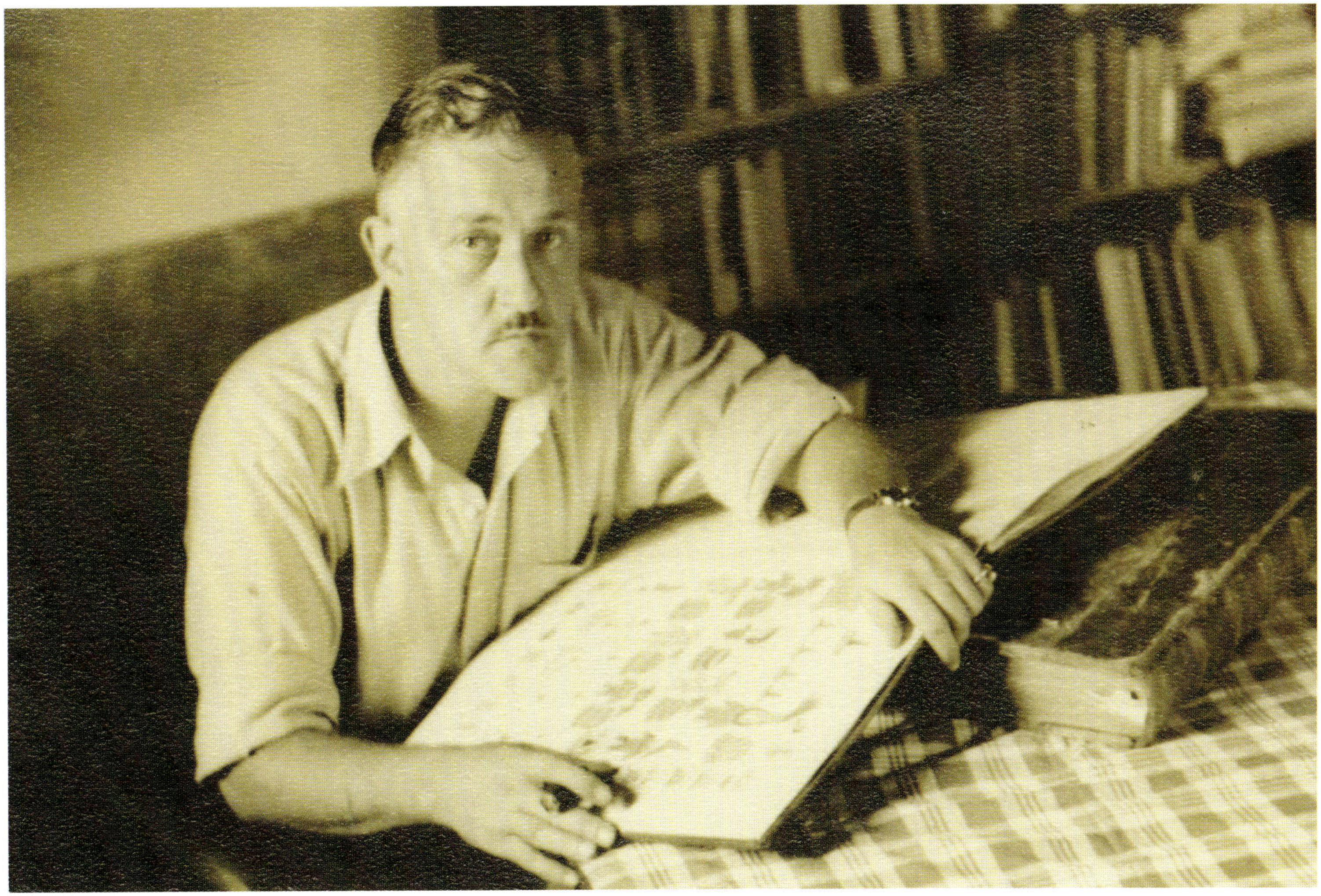

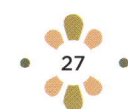

Photograph of William Spratling Holding a Design Album, u.d.
Gelatin silver print
The Latin American Library, Tulane University
Spratling-Taxco Collection

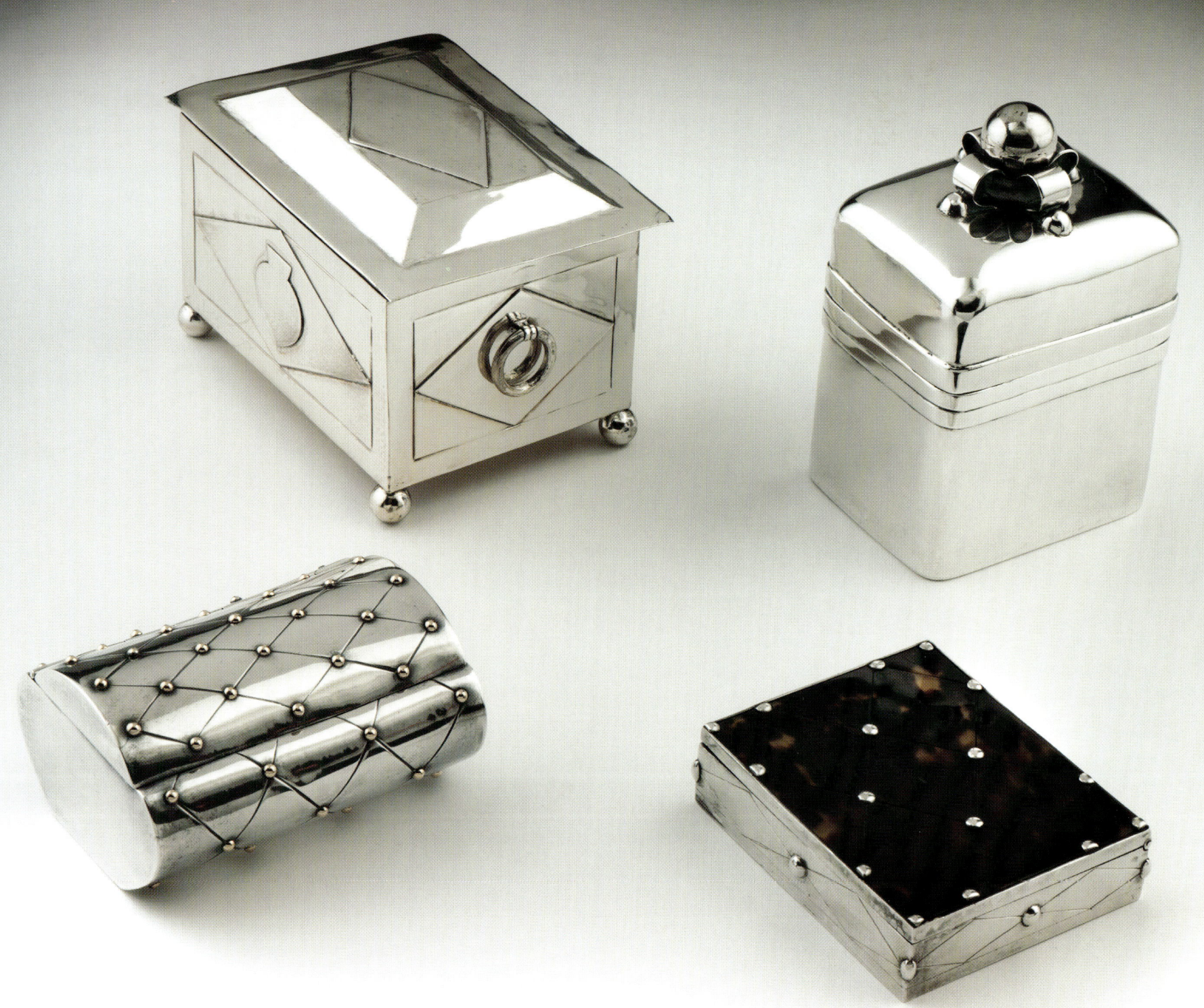

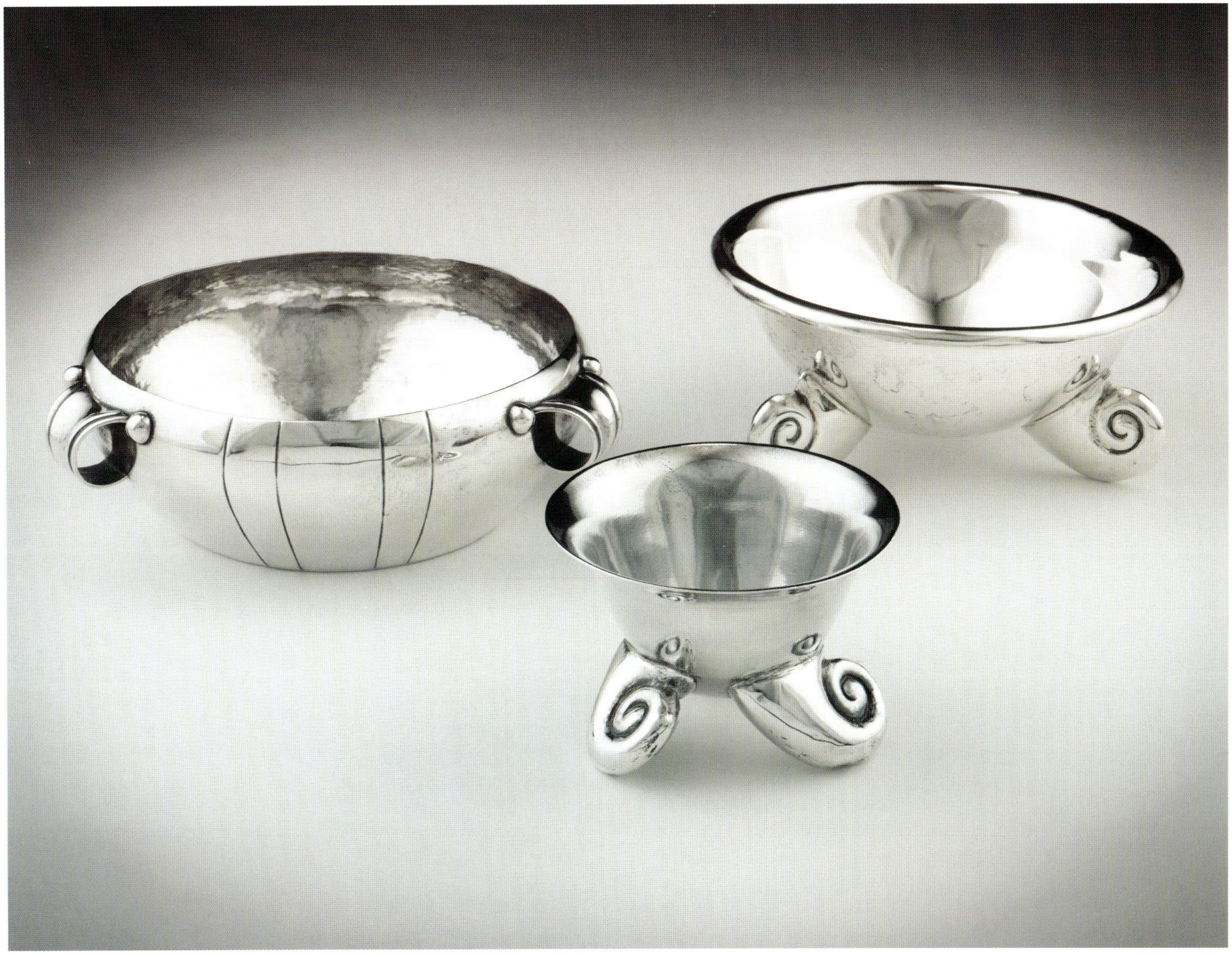

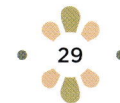

29

Opposite:
WILLIAM SPRATLING
Silver Boxes, c. 1940s
Silver and tortoiseshell
Collection of Don Fuson
Photo © David Humphreys, 2015

Above:
WILLIAM SPRATLING
Silver Bowls, c. 1940s
Silver and tortoiseshell
Collection of Don Fuson
Photo © David Humphreys, 2015

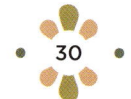

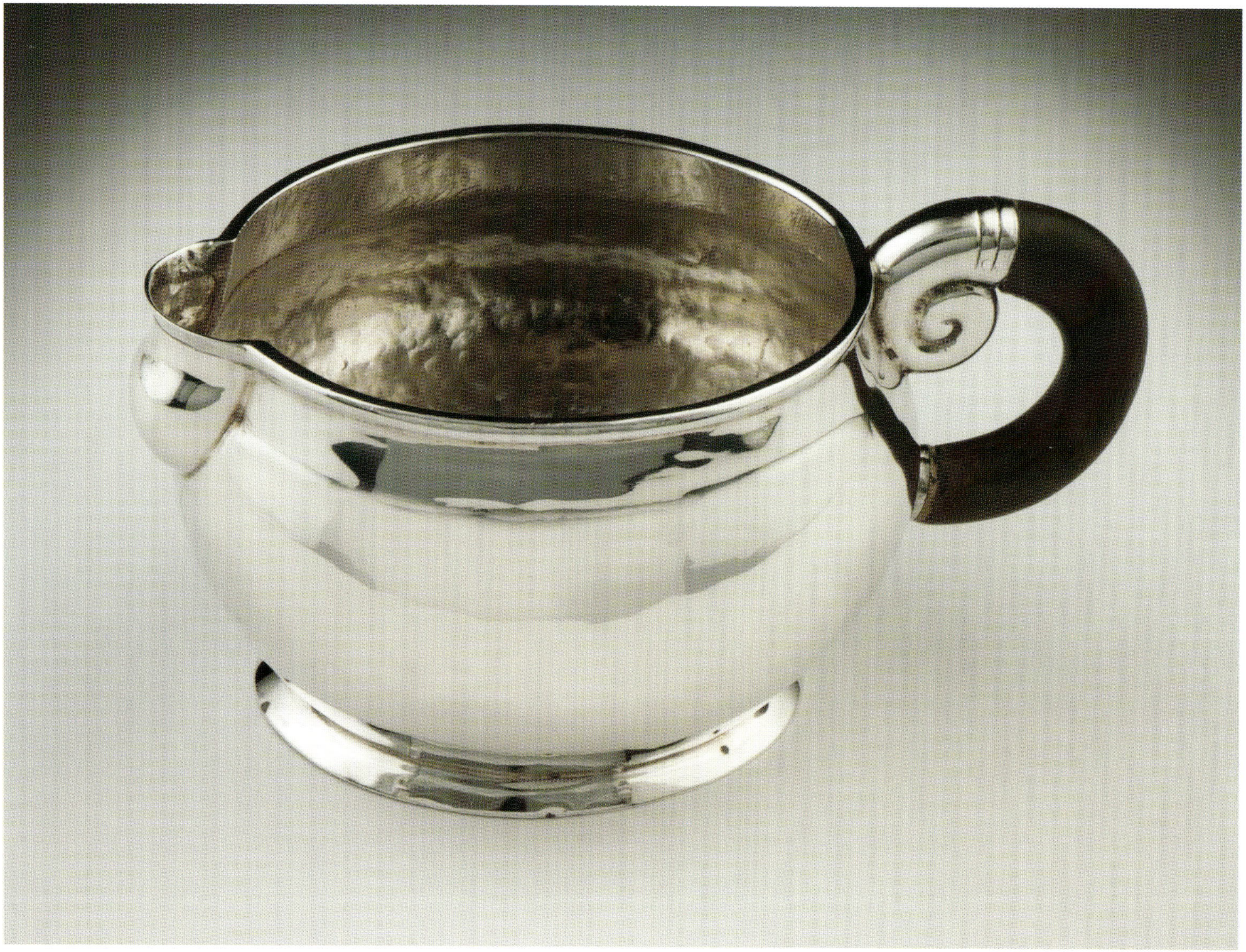

WILLIAM SPRATLING
Cream Pitcher, c. 1931-45
Sterling silver and rosewood
LSU Museum of Art, 96.10
Gift of the Friends of LSU Museum of Art
Photo © David Humphreys, 2015

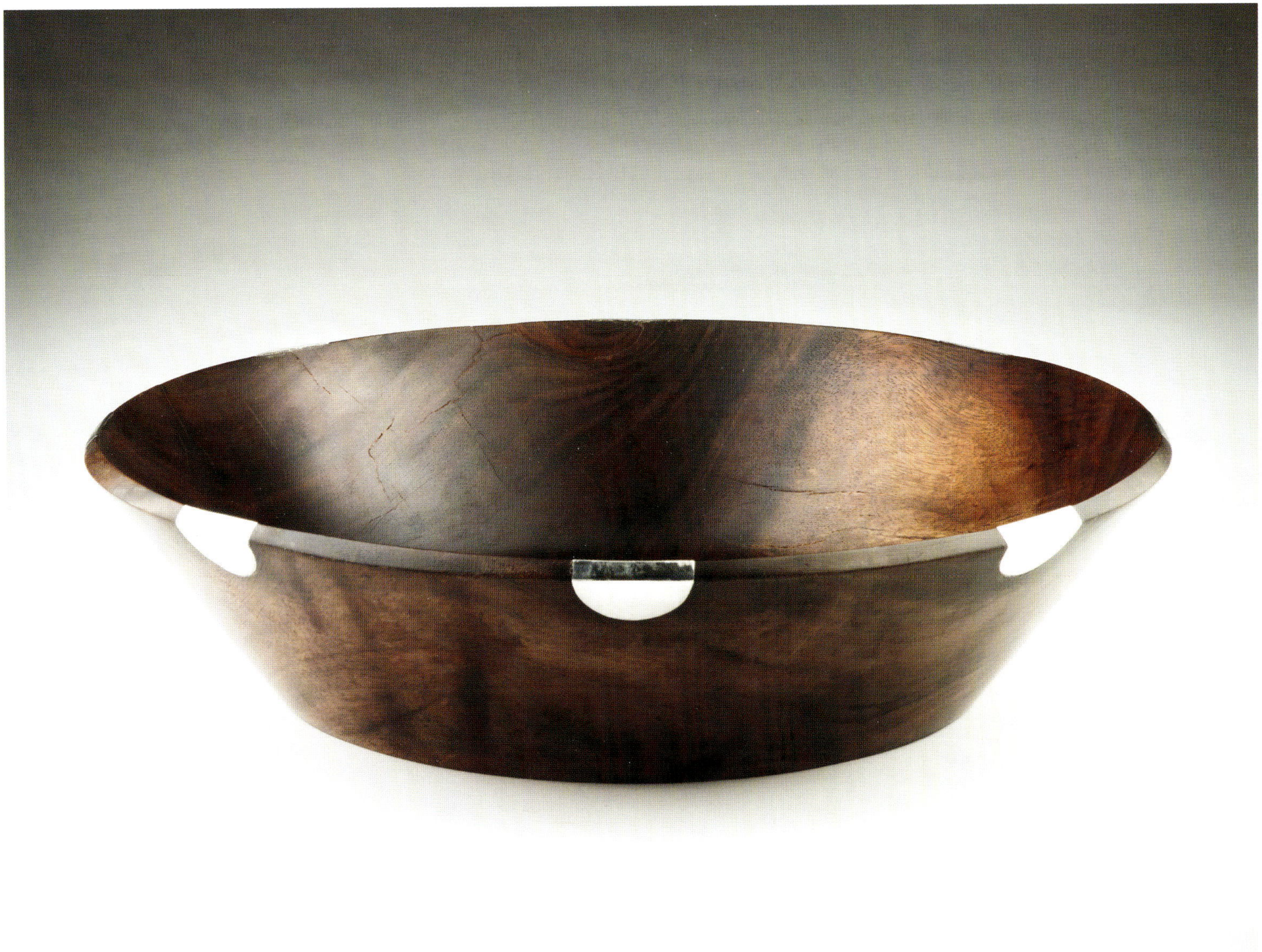

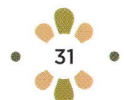

William Spratling
Wood and Silver Bowl, c. 1940s
Wood and silver
Collection of Don Fuson
Photo © David Humphreys, 2015

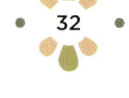

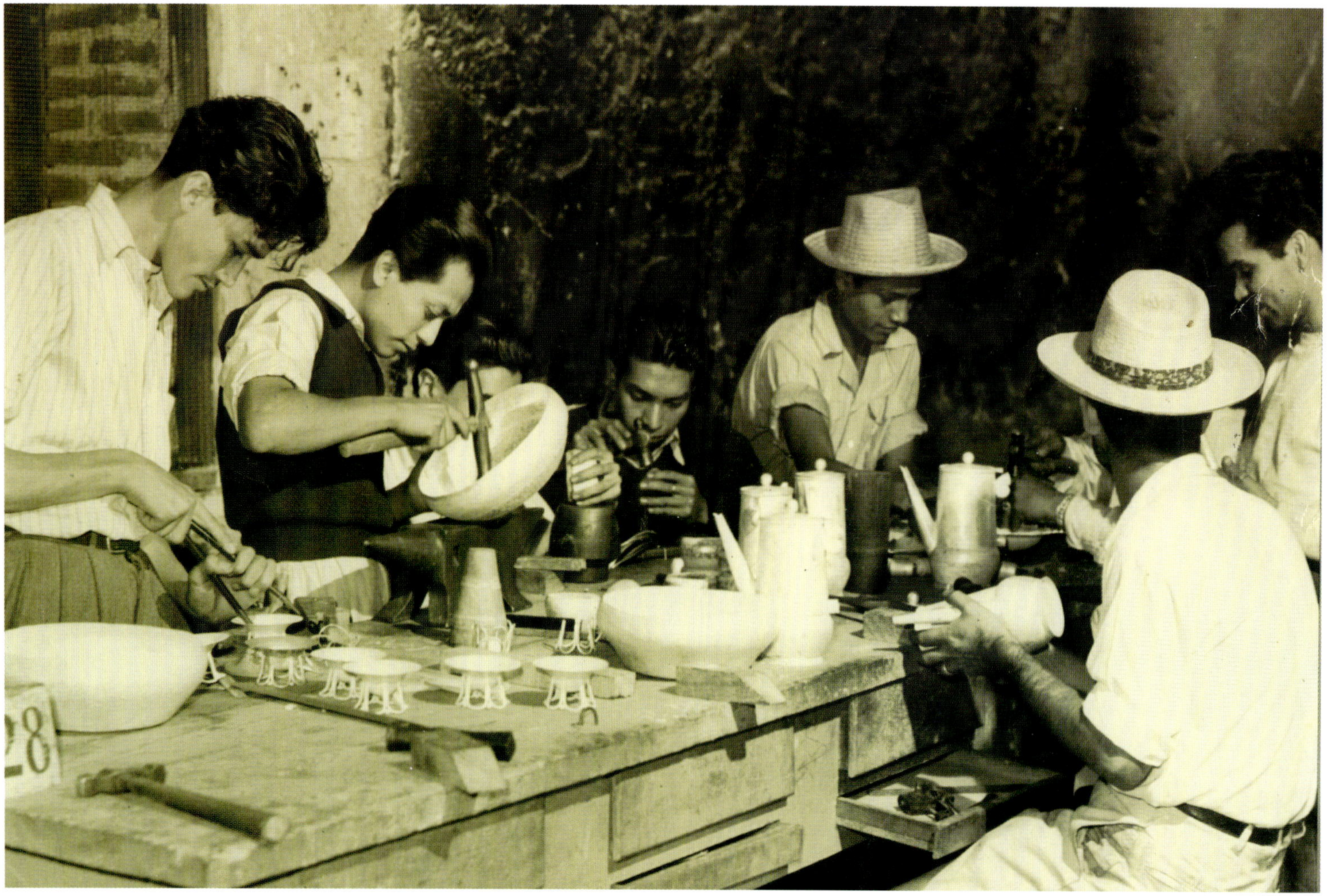

Photograph of William Spratling's Studio in Taxco, Mexico, c. 1940s
Gelatin silver print
The Latin American Library, Tulane University
Spratling-Taxco Collection

In addition to ancient art, Spratling was also strongly influenced by the work of contemporary Mexican artists and artisans. Spratling worked closely with Mexican artists and designers in his silver workshop and studio, and was instrumental in the revival of Mexican silversmithing traditions in the 1920s and 1930s. The Los Castillo designers were a group of Mexican artisans that apprenticed with Spratling and went on to form a hugely influential silver workshop that produced jewelry and decorative art objects wildly popular in both the United States and Mexico. Many of the most important Mexican artists and silversmiths of this period, like Don Antonio Castillo, began their careers as apprentices in his workshop.

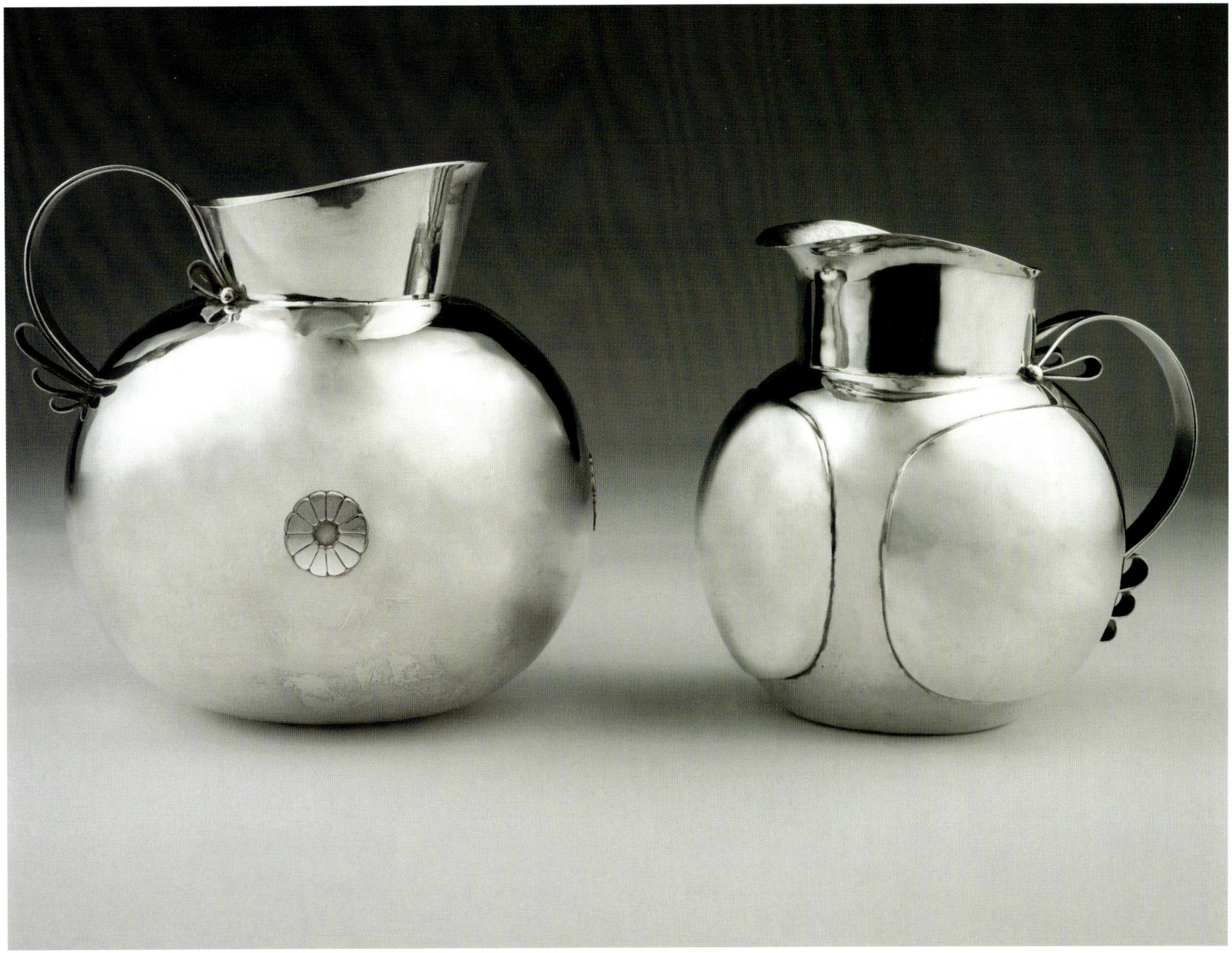

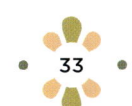

William Spratling
Silver Pitchers, c. 1940s
Silver
Collection of Don Fuson
Photo © David Humphreys, 2015

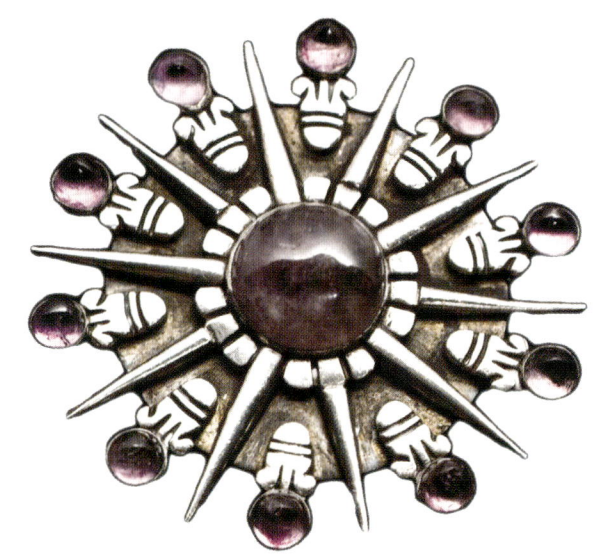

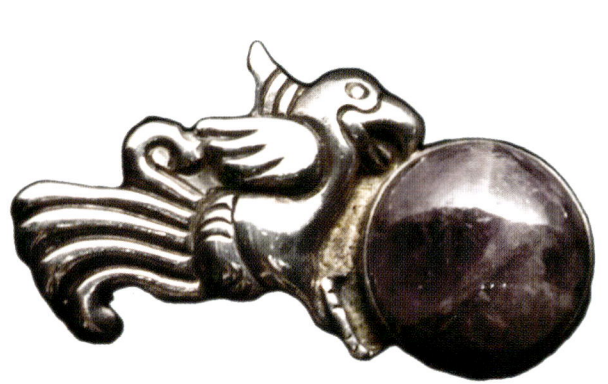

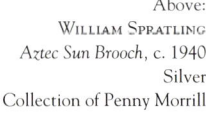

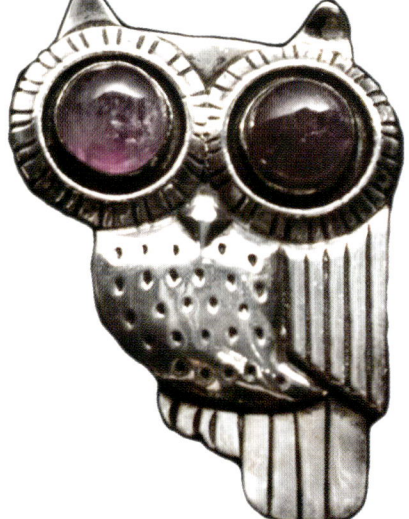

Above:
WILLIAM SPRATLING
Aztec Sun Brooch, c. 1940
Silver
Collection of Penny Morrill

Above:
WILLIAM SPRATLING
Parrot Brooch, c. 1940
Silver with amethyst cabochon
Collection of Penny Morrill

Above:
WILLIAM SPRATLING
Owl Brooch, c. 1940
Silver with amethyst quartz cabochons
Collection of Penny Morrill

Opposite:
WILLIAM SPRATLING
Silver Tray, c. 1940s
Silver with amethyst quartz cabochons
Collection of Don Fuson
Photo © David Humphreys, 2015

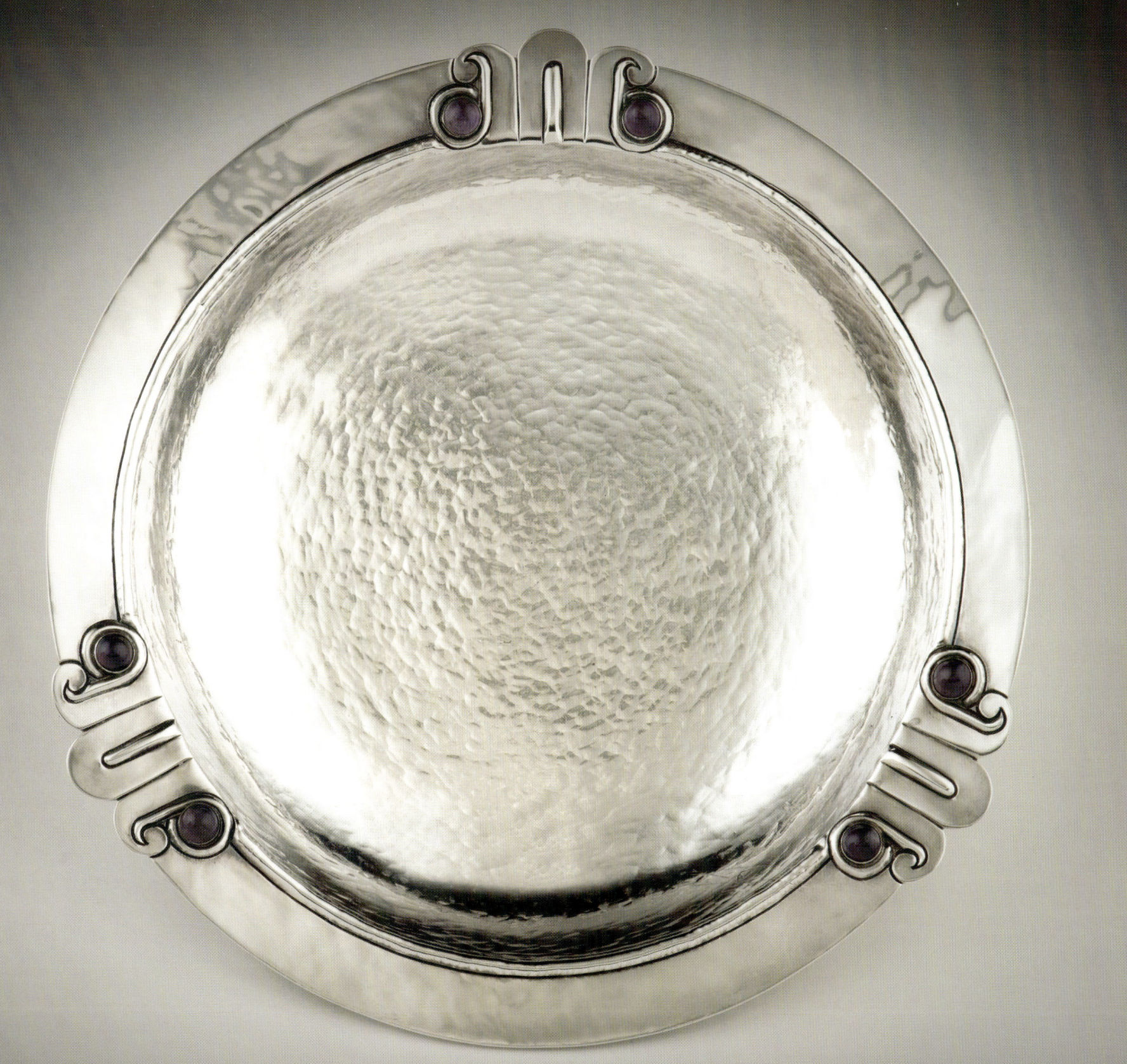

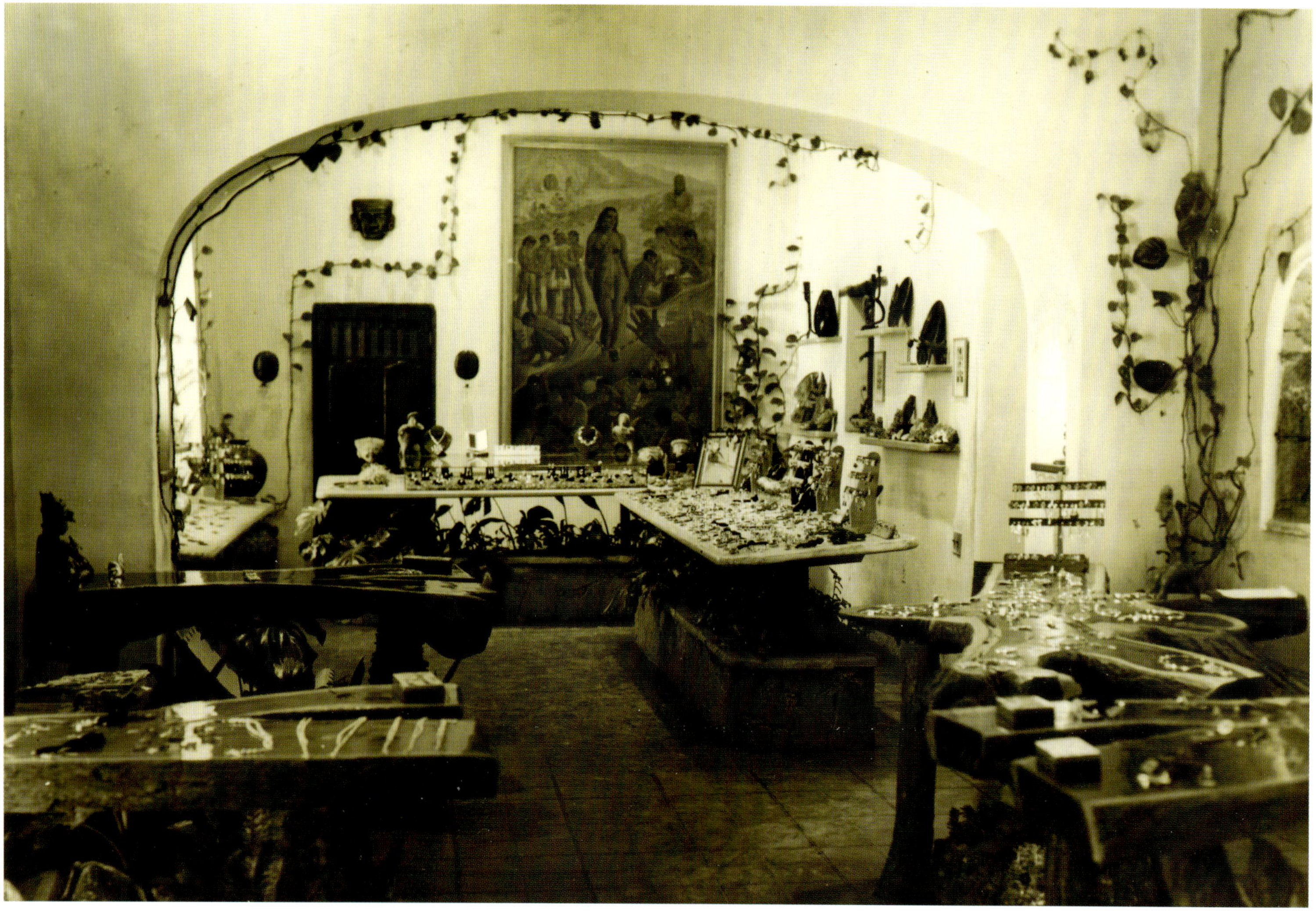

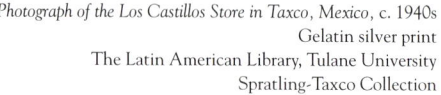

Photograph of the Los Castillos Store in Taxco, Mexico, c. 1940s
Gelatin silver print
The Latin American Library, Tulane University
Spratling-Taxco Collection

 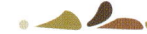

The Los Castillo silver company was founded by Mexican designer Don Antonio Castillo in 1939. Castillo was an apprentice in William Spratling's silver workshop as a teenager, and became one of Mexico's finest silver designers. The Los Castillo workshop supported and sold the work of many of Mexico's top artisans, including Hector Aguilar, Margot van Voorhies Carr, and Antonio Pineda, and continues to serve an integral role in the preservation of the Mexican silver traditions.

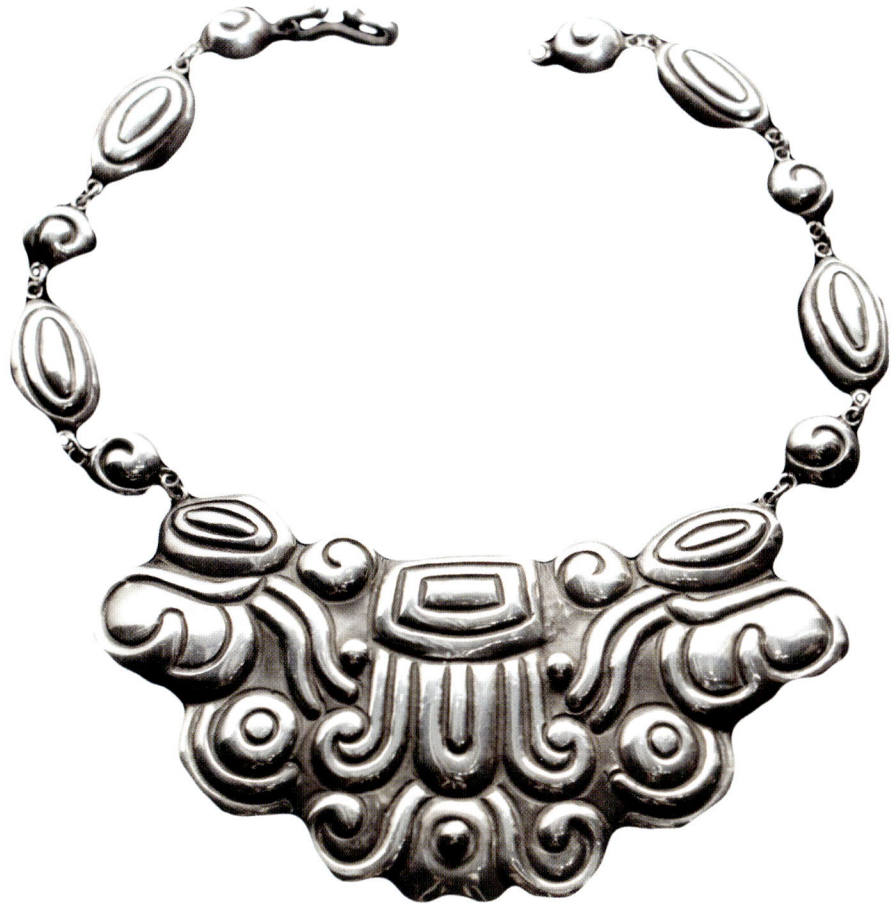

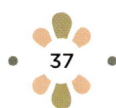

Margot Van Voorhies Castillo
Los Castillo Ce Acatl Necklace, c. 1939-40
Silver
Collection of Penny Morrill

After moving to Mexico in 1937 and marrying Don Antonio Castillo, the American-born silver designer Margot Van Voorhies Castillo, who went by "Margot de Taxco," became one of the strongest voices in Mexican silver design. Many early Los Castillo designs reflect her influence, and, after divorcing Don Antonio Castillo in 1948, she opened her own studio and shop. She had a strong interest in ancient Aztec art and culture, and often used Aztec signs and symbols in her designs, as in this necklace, which features a pattern taken from the date glyph that appears at the center of the Aztec calendar stone.

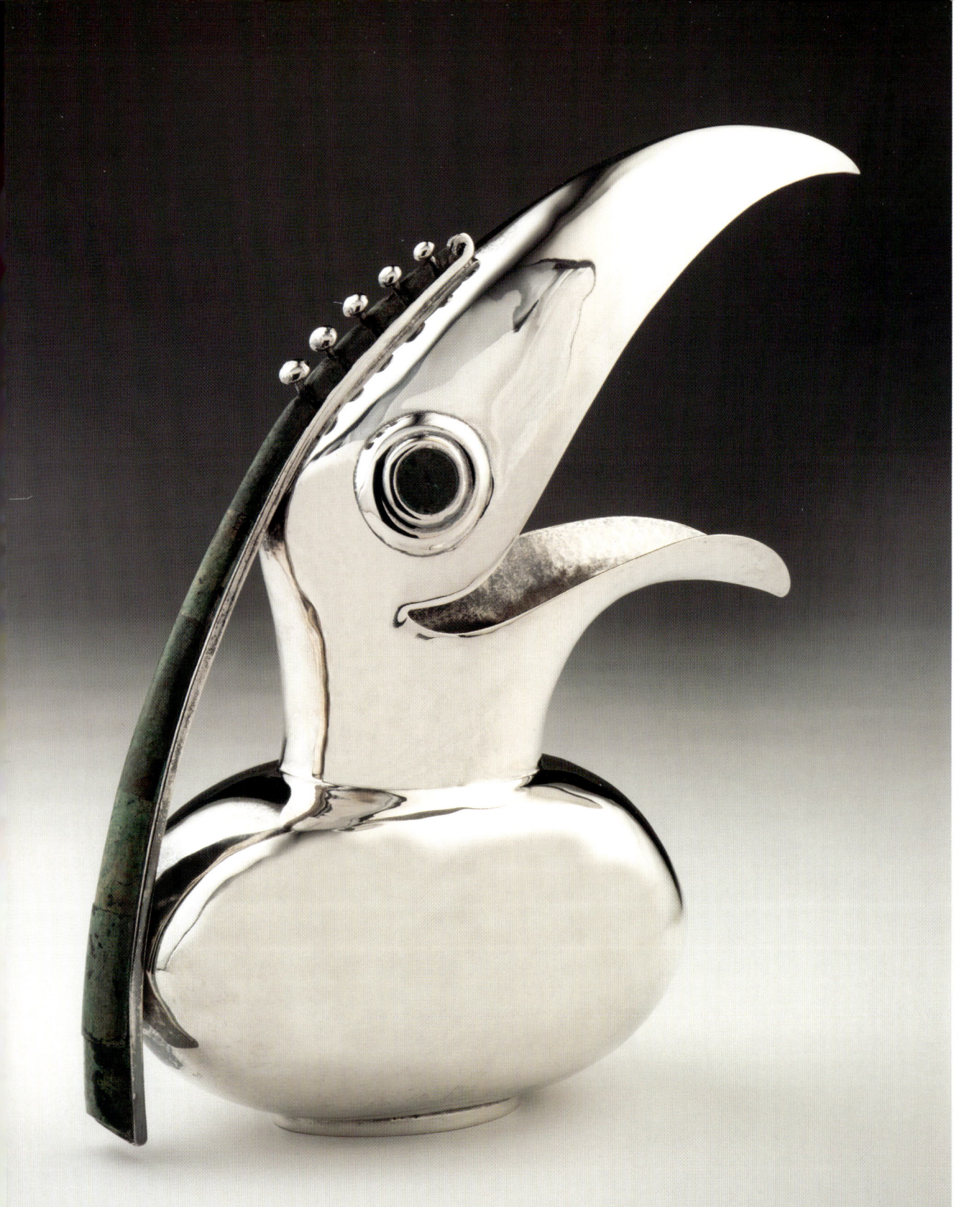

LOS CASTILLO
Los Castillo Silver Pitcher with Bird, c. 1950s
Silver with green turquoise
Collection of Shanna Boudreaux
Photo © David Humphreys, 2015

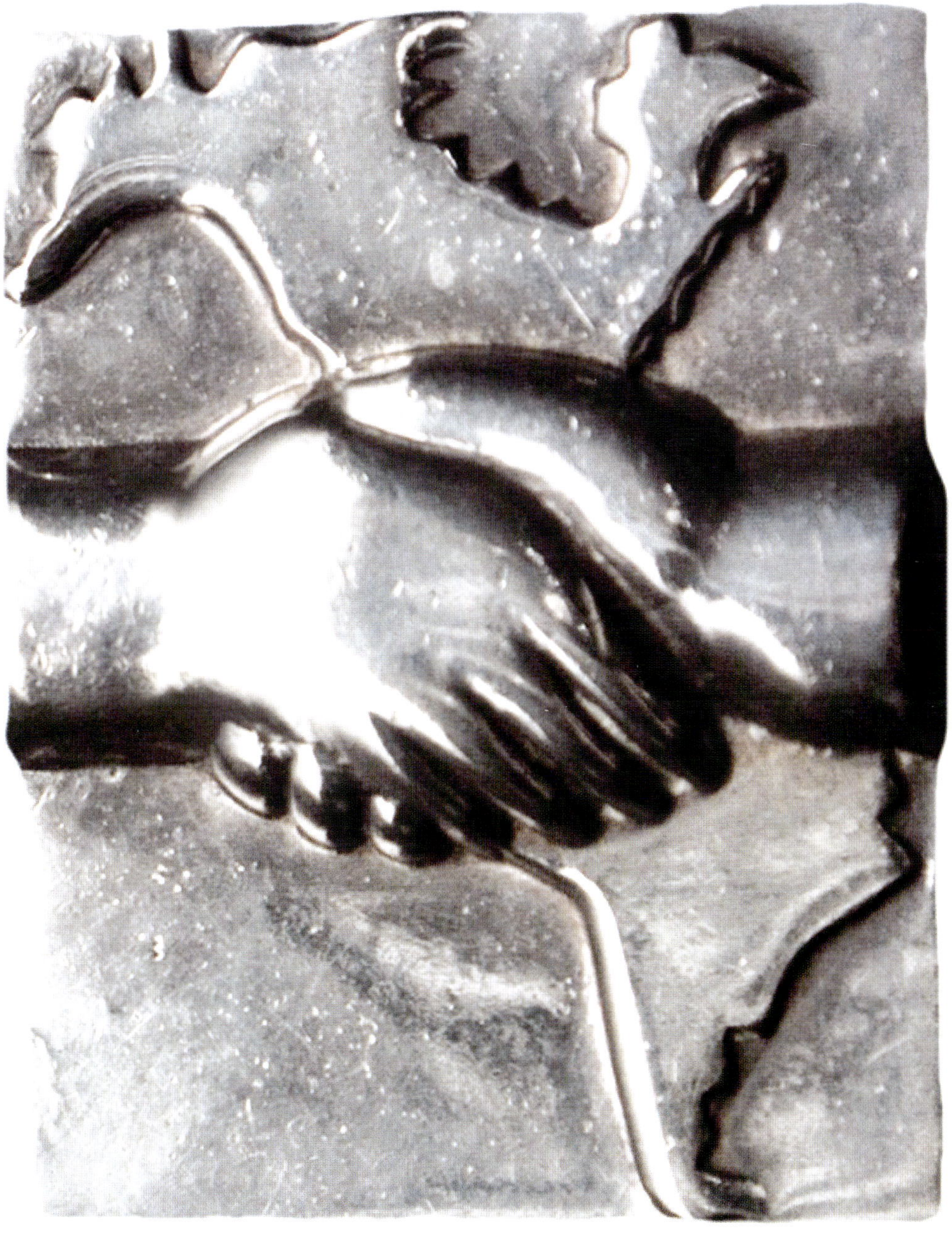

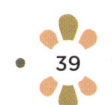

WILLIAM SPRATLING
Hands Across America Brooch, 1942
Silver
Collection of Penny Morrill

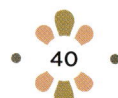

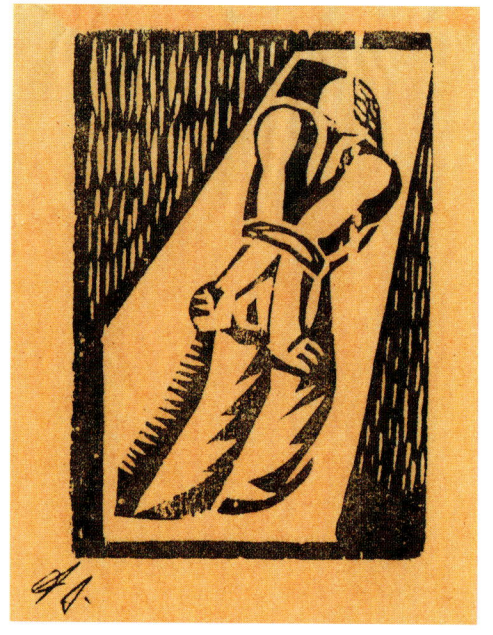 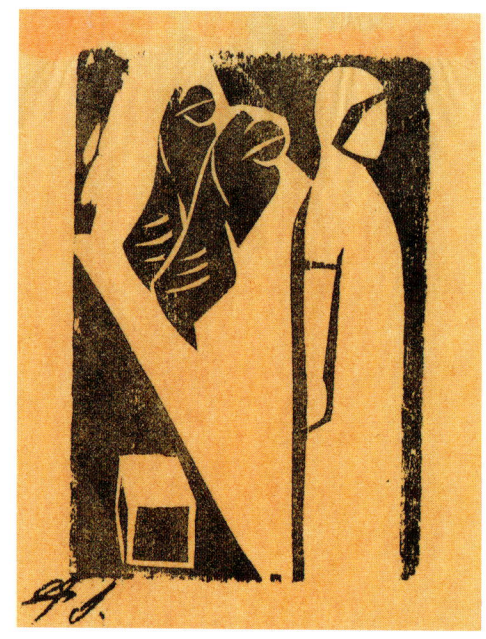 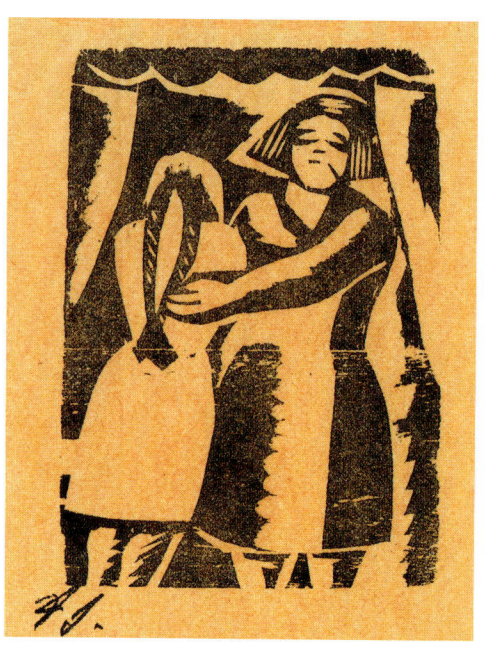

DAVID ALFARO SIQUEIROS
13 Grabados en Madera por Siqueiros, Taxco, 1931 (printed 1992)
Portfolio of 13 woodcuts (12 printed on orange paper and one printed on lavender paper)
The Latin American Library, Tulane University
Spratling-Taxco Collection
©2015 Banco de México Diego Rivera Frida Kahlo Museums Trust,
México, D.F./Artist Rights Society (ARS), New York

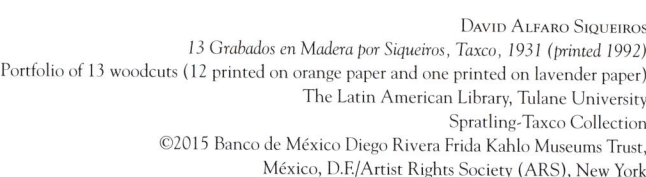

While imprisoned in Mexico as a political dissident, Siqueiros produced the book *13 Grabados,* which contained a series of 13 woodcut prints that Siqueiros published alongside an introduction by Spratling in 1931. In Spratling's introduction, he praised Siqueiros for his astonishingly modern economy of form, which Spratling saw as inspired by the simple, graphic forms of Pre-Columbian art, whose influence transformed these works into a bold and hugely effective political statement.

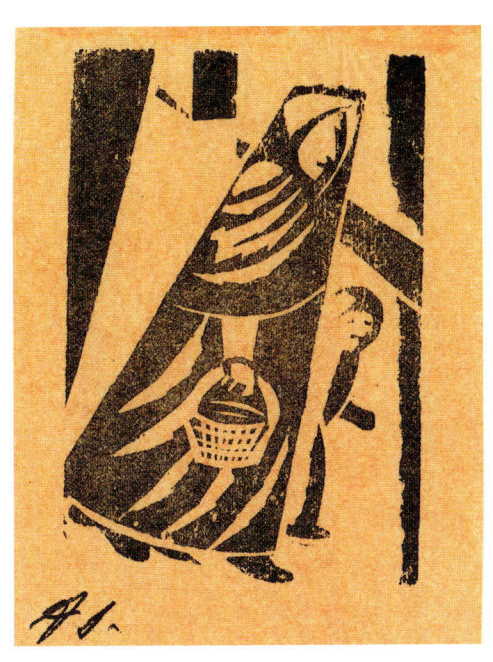
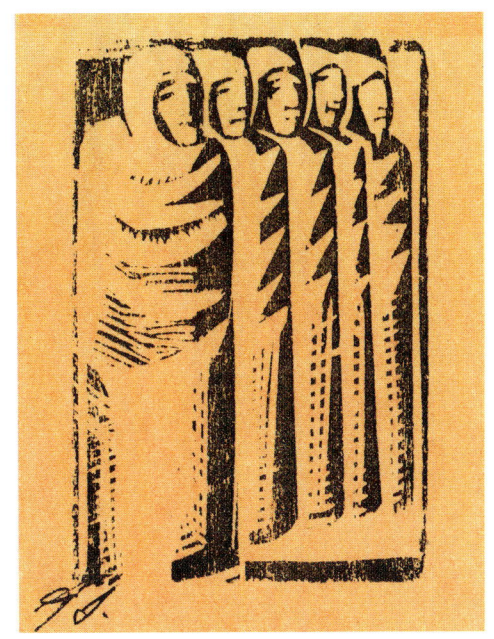
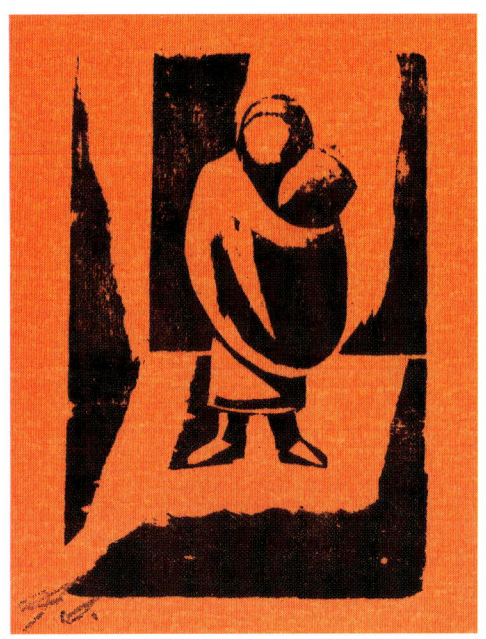

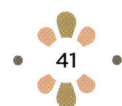

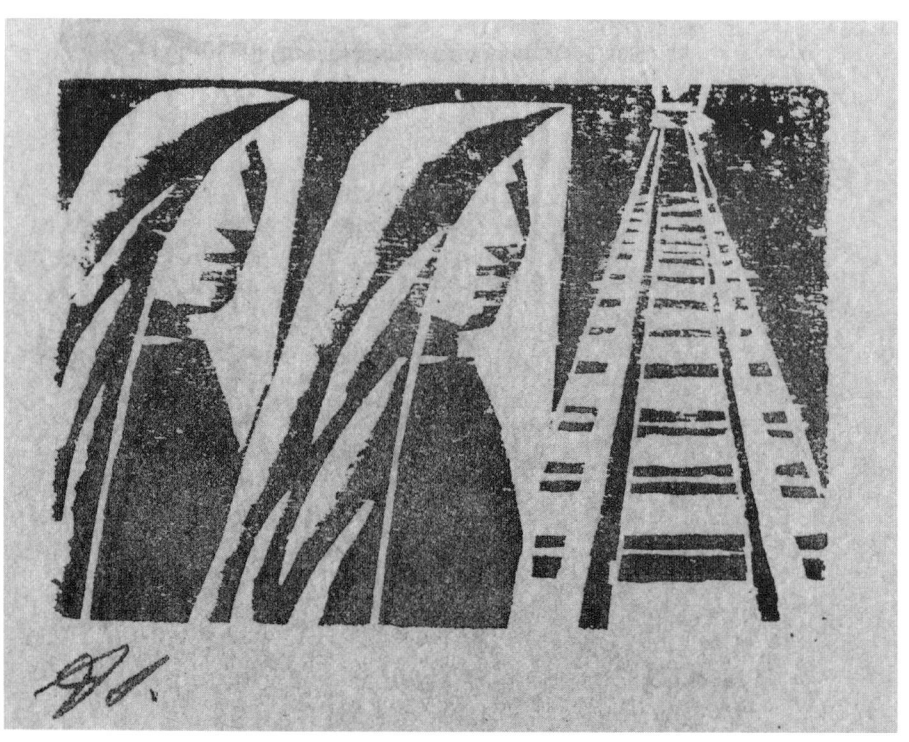

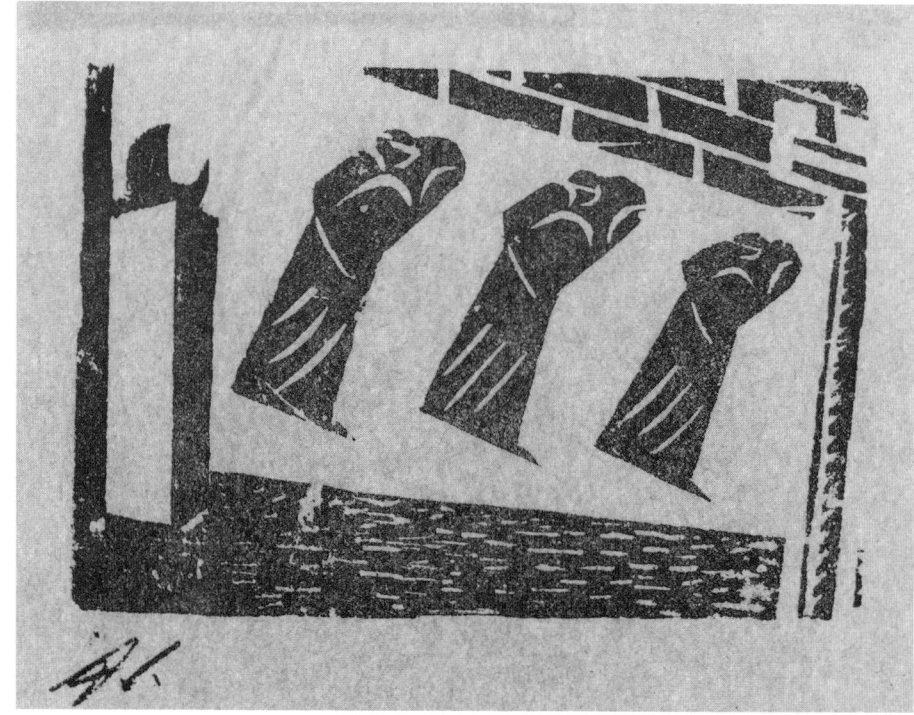

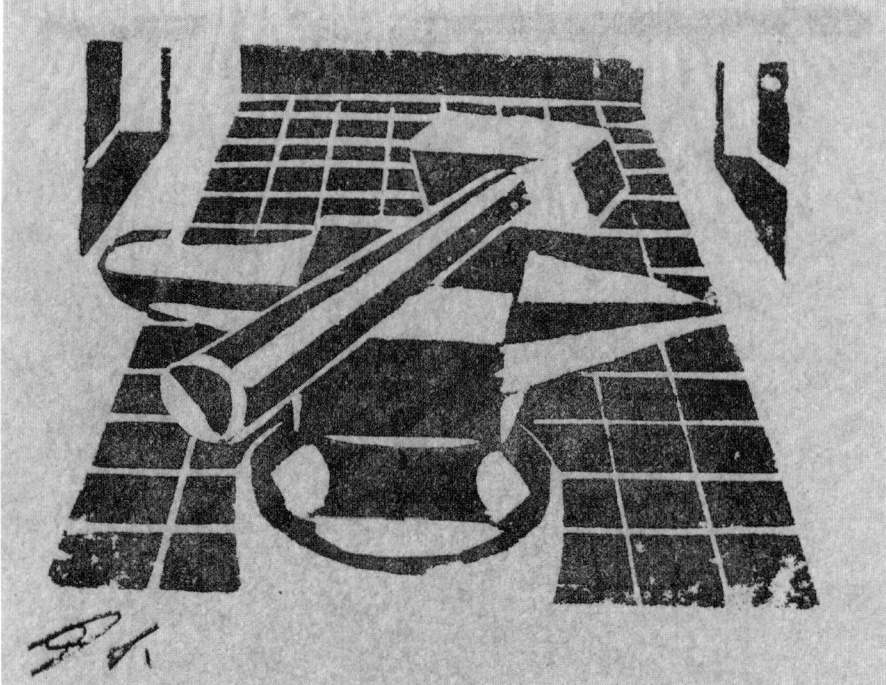

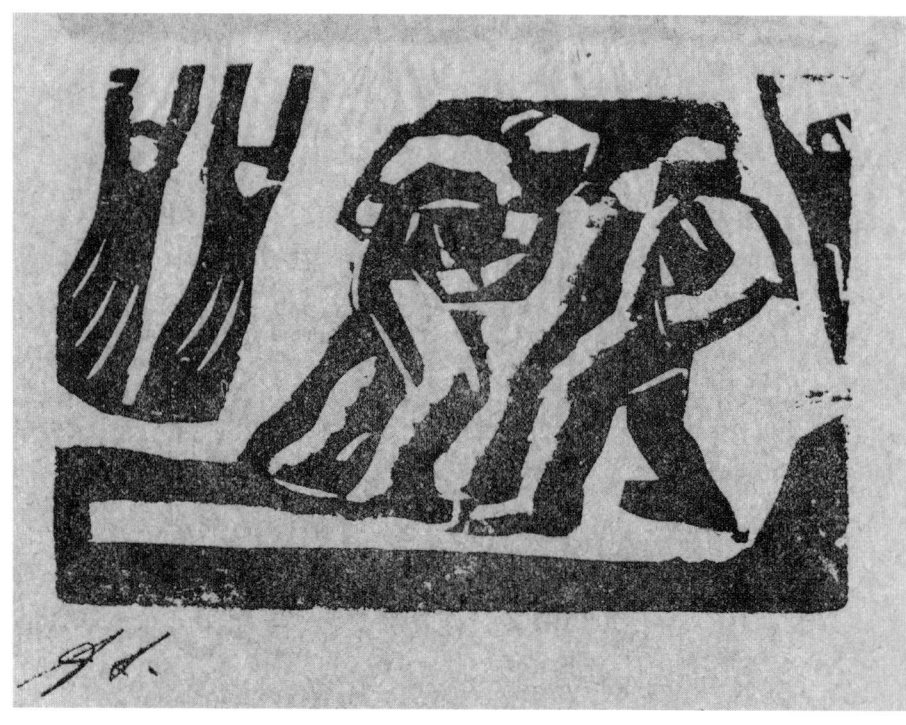

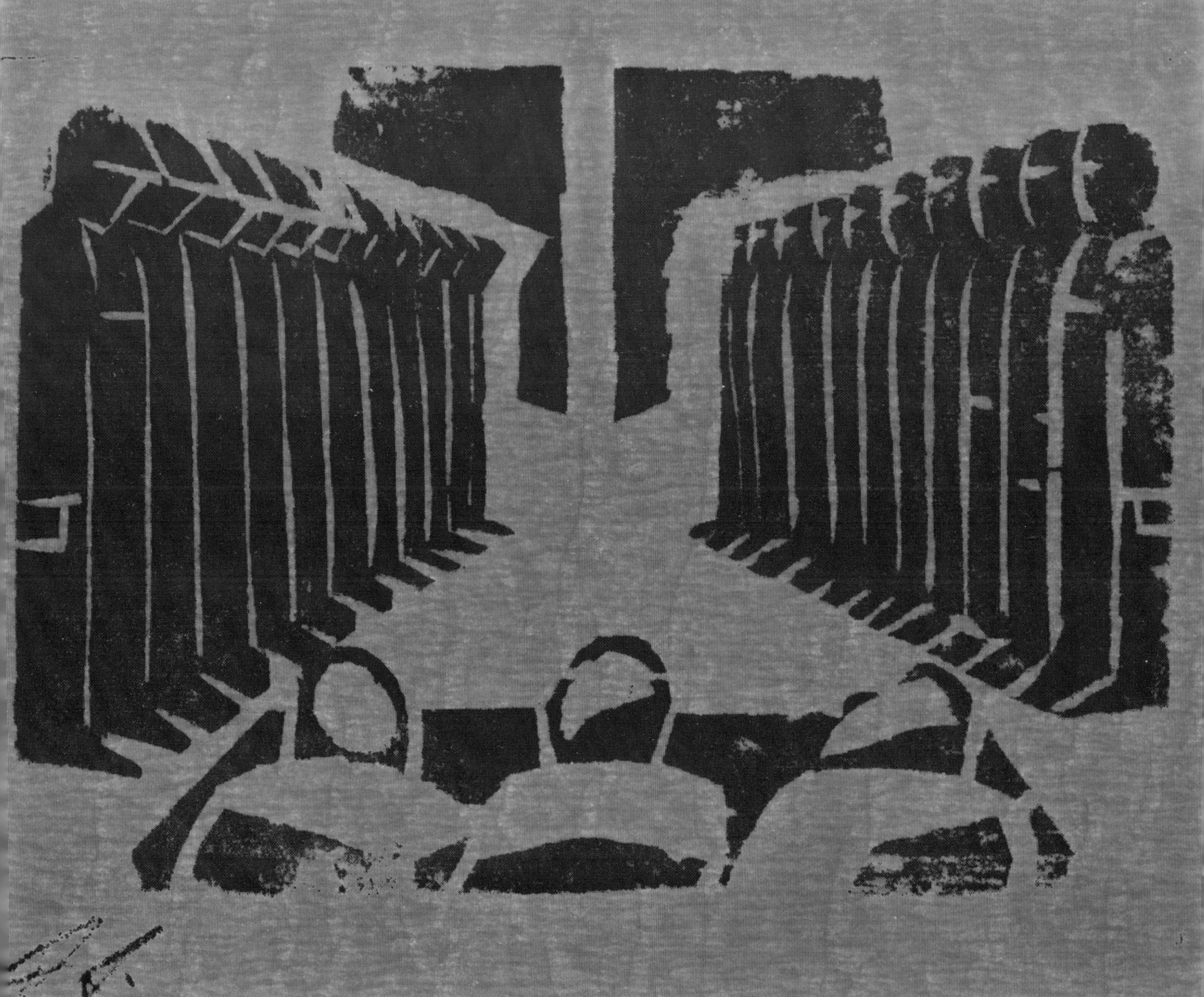

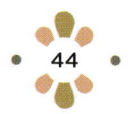

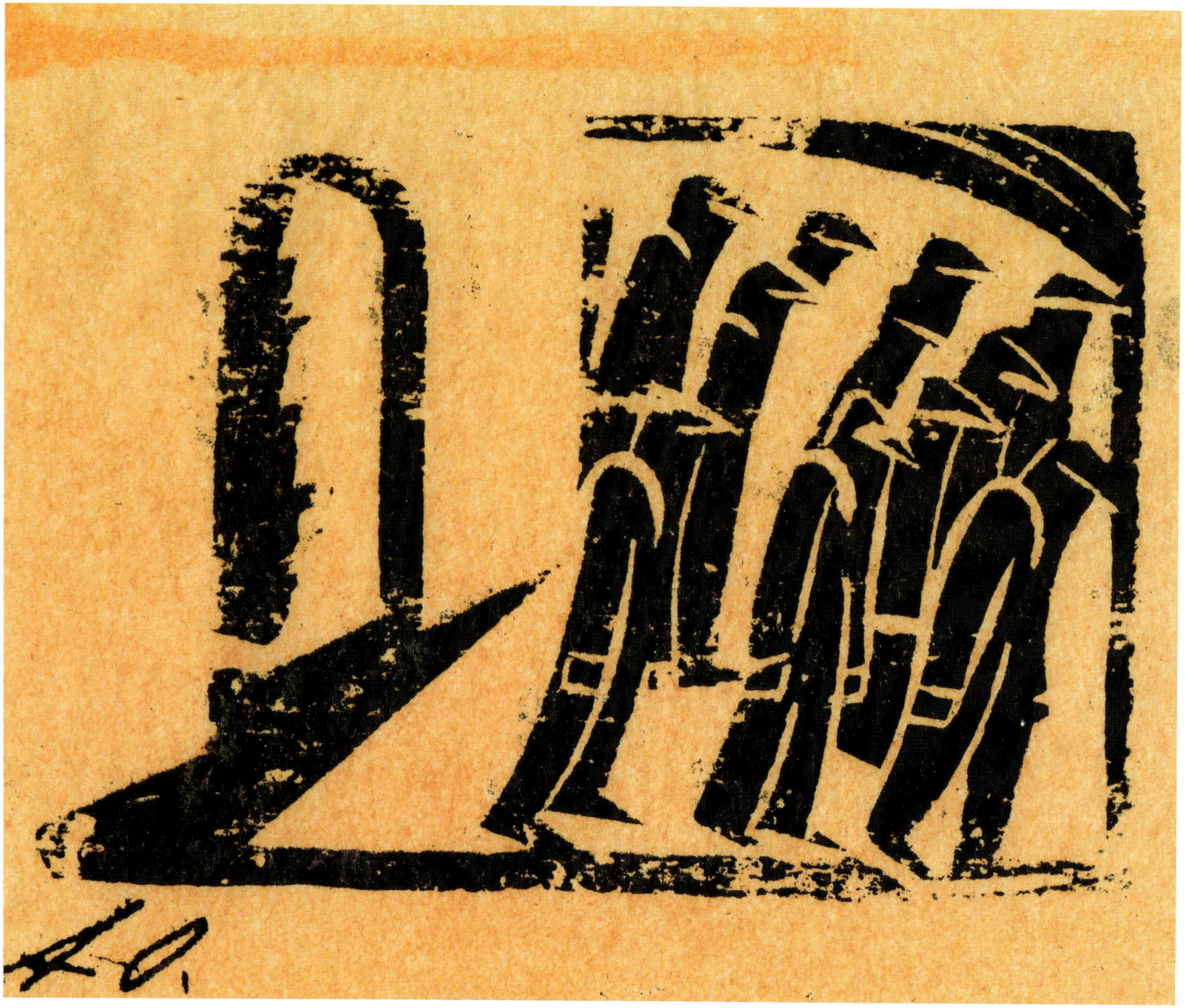

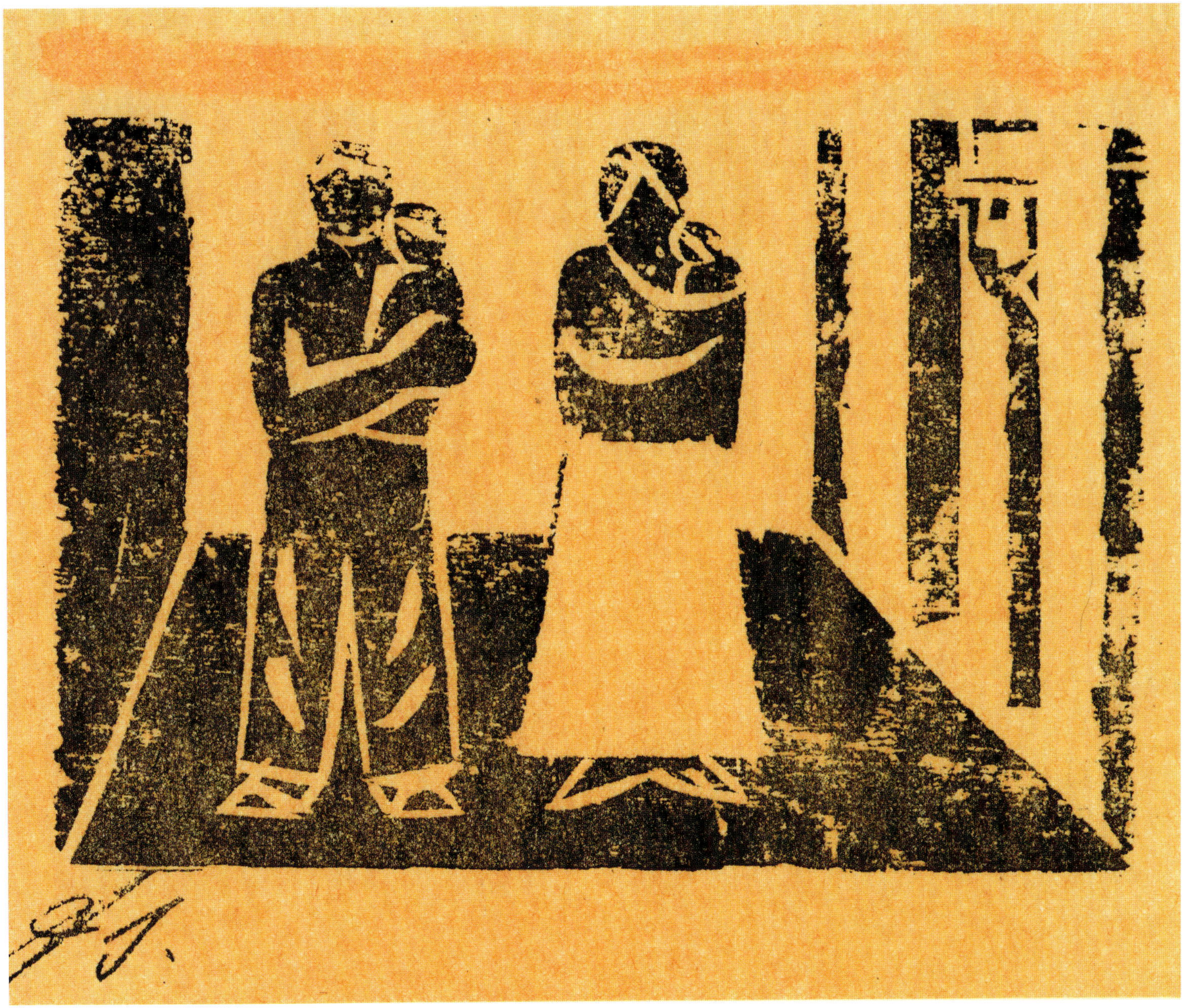

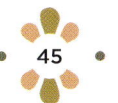

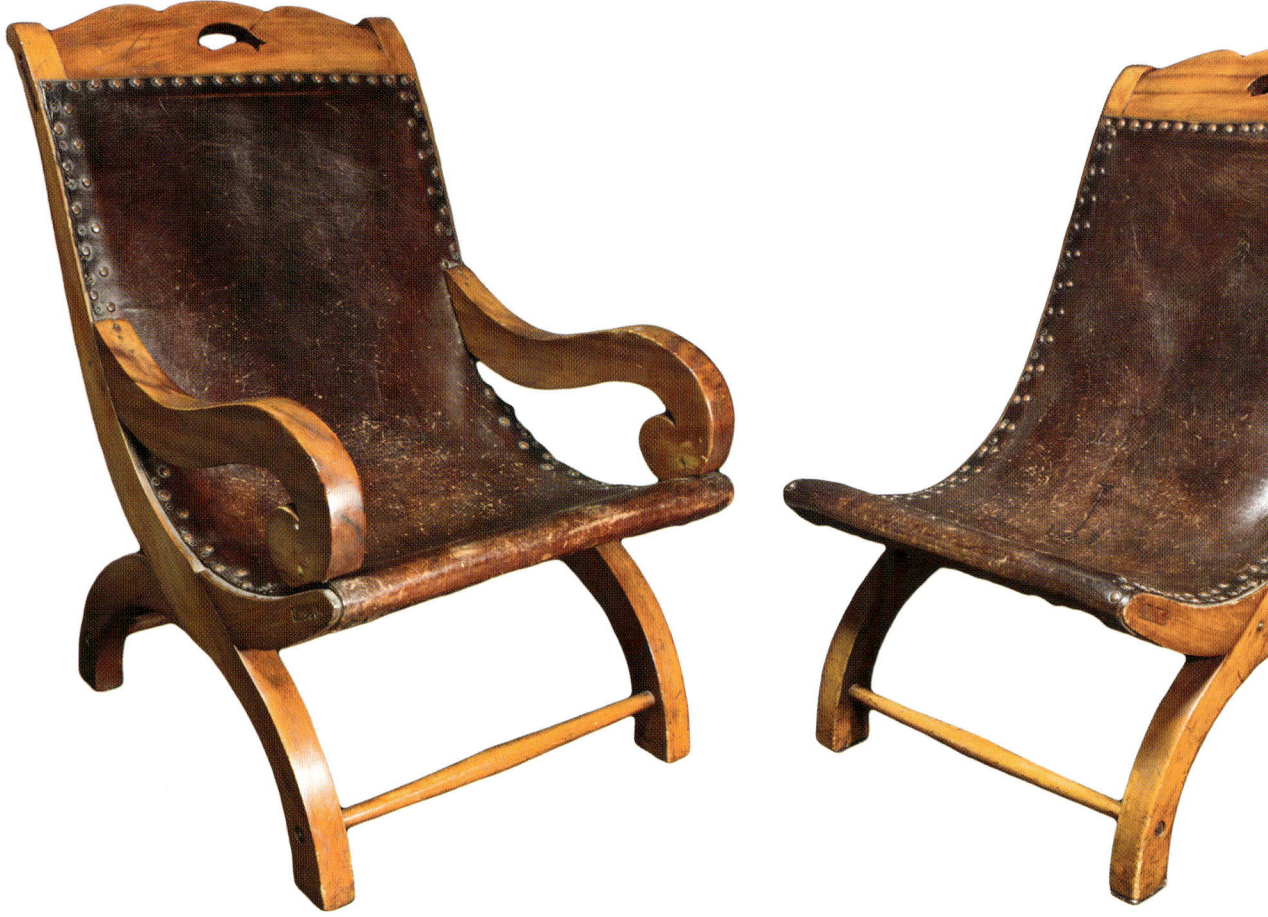

WILLIAM SPRATLING
2 Campeche Chairs, c. 1930s
Wood and leather
Collection of Caroline Wogan Sontheimer and Stephen Louis Sontheimer

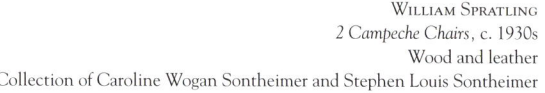

The campeche chair was a fixture of 19th-century American plantation life and is an example of the strong historical connections between Latin America, the Caribbean and the American South. The style originated in Mexico's Yucatan Penninsula in the 18th century and was widely in use throughout the American South, and especially Louisiana, in the 18th and 19th centuries. Spratling made these modern reinterpretations of the campeche chair for Caroline Durieux's family, and they remain in the home of her descendants today.

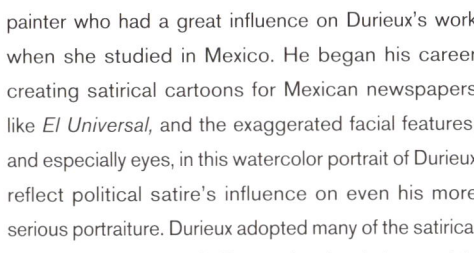

Carlos Orozco Romero was a Mexican cartoonist and painter who had a great influence on Durieux's work when she studied in Mexico. He began his career creating satirical cartoons for Mexican newspapers like *El Universal,* and the exaggerated facial features, and especially eyes, in this watercolor portrait of Durieux reflect political satire's influence on even his more serious portraiture. Durieux adopted many of the satirical strategies in evidence in Romero's prints in her work in Mexico as well as her work in New Orleans.

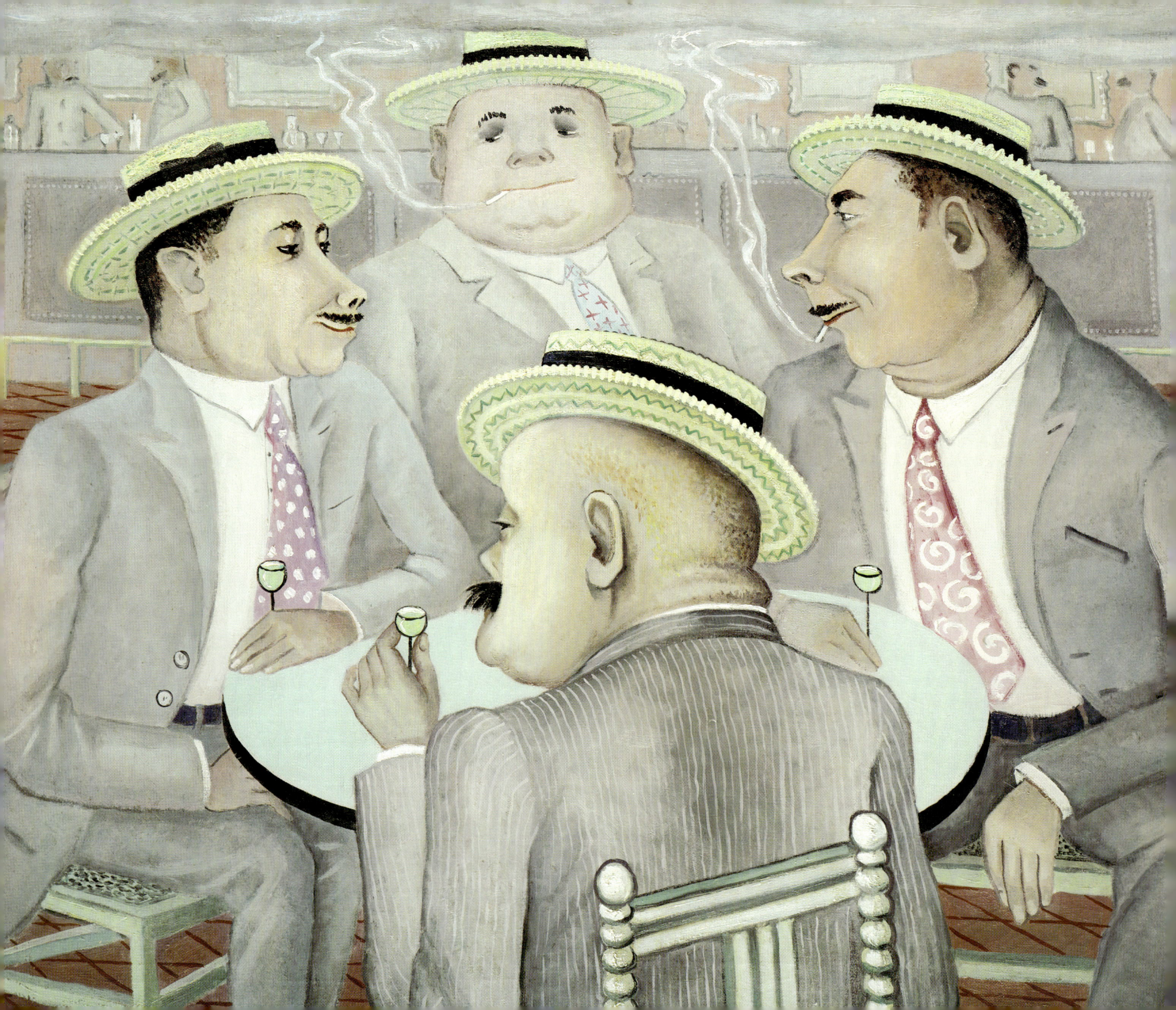

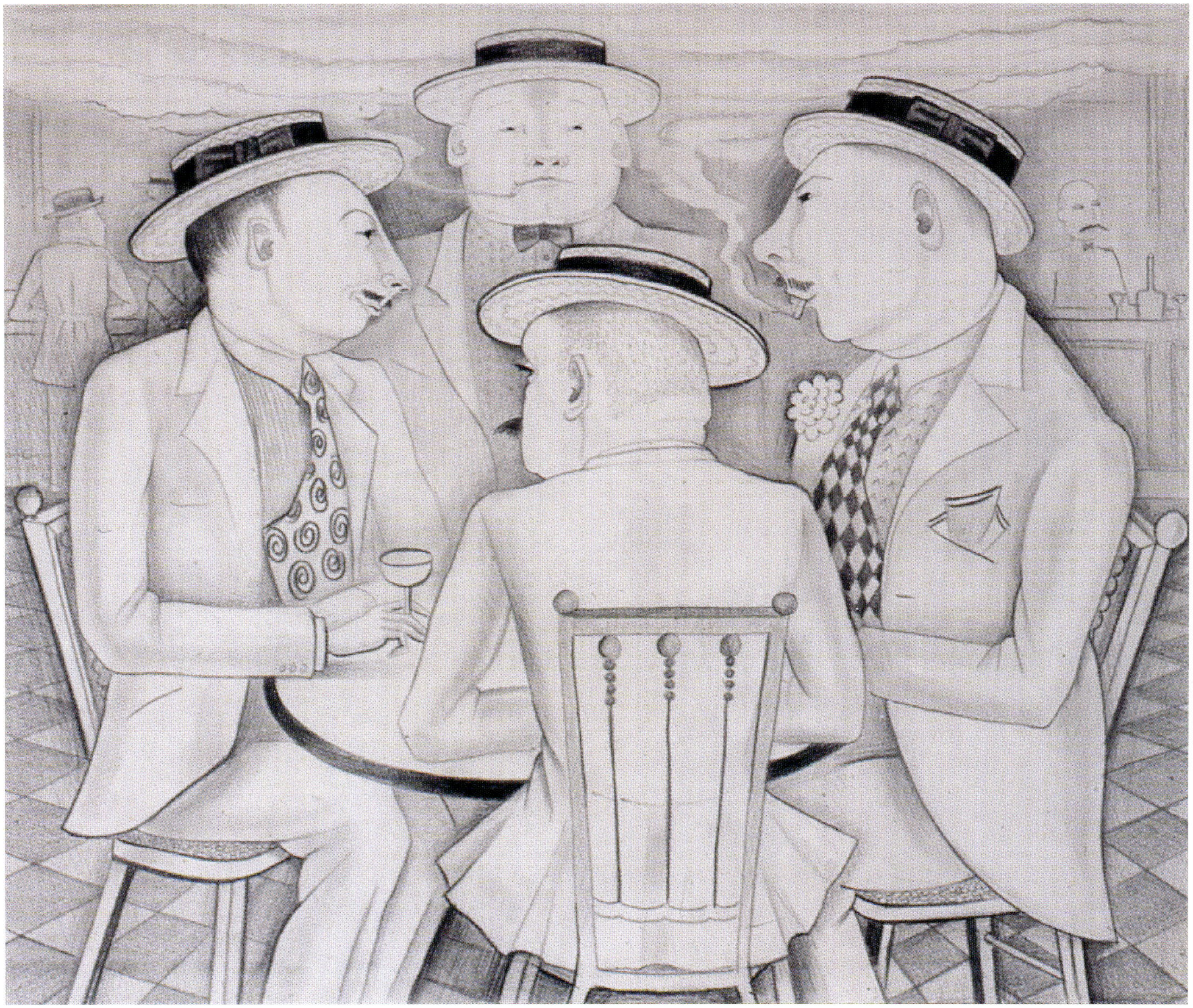

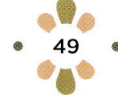

49

Opposite:
CAROLINE WOGAN DURIEUX
Café Tupinamba, 1934
Oil on canvas
LSU Museum of Art, 91.25
Gift of Mr. Charles P. Manship, Jr.; Conservation with funds provided by Ms. Nadine Carter Russell

Above:
CAROLINE WOGAN DURIEUX
Cartoon Drawing for Café Tupinamba, c. 1934
Lithograph on paper
LSU Museum of Art, 91.26
Gift of the Friends of LSU Museum of Art

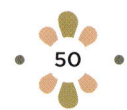

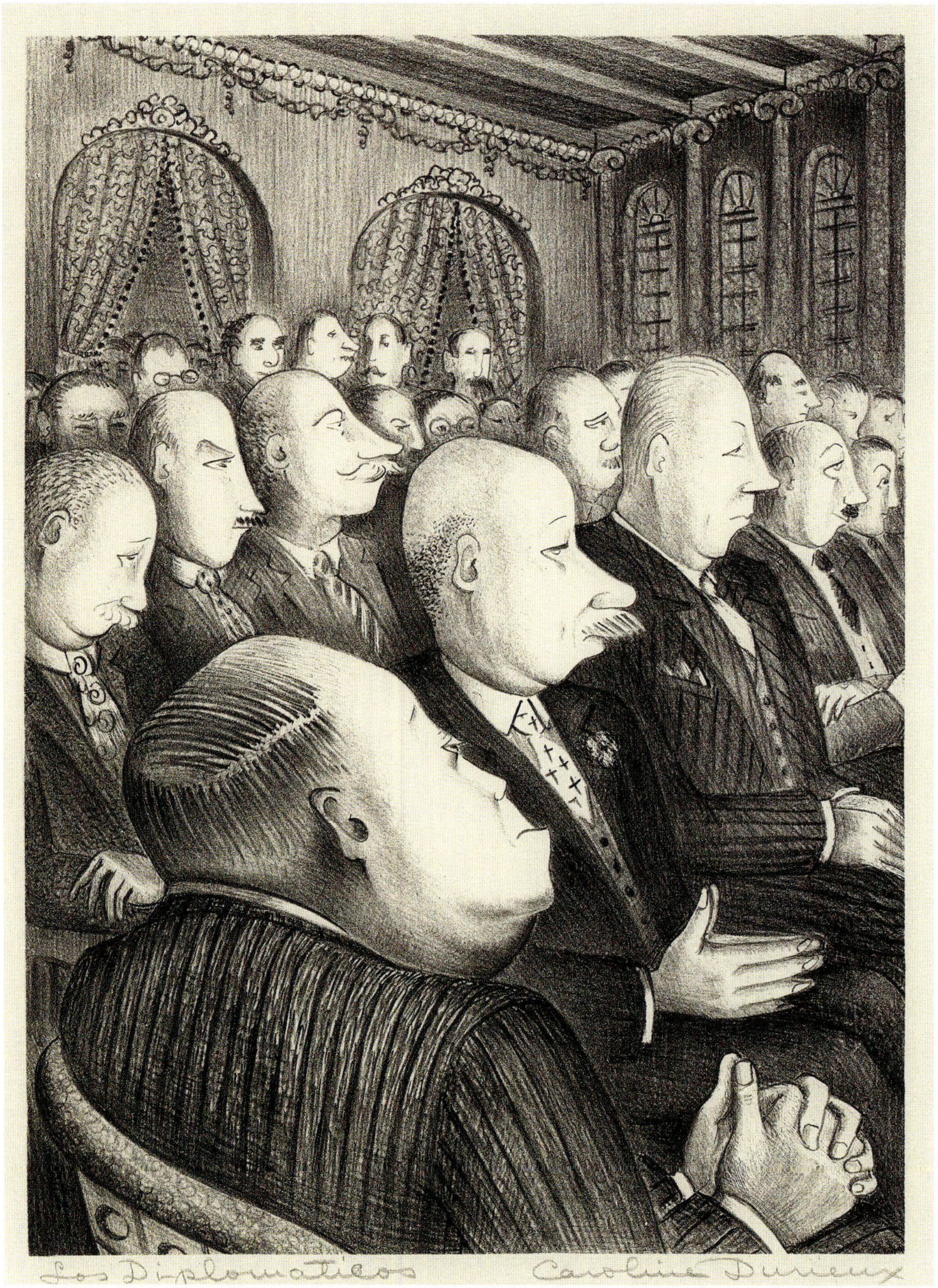

Los Diplomáticos   Caroline Durieux

Left:
CAROLINE WOGAN DURIEUX
Los Diplomáticos, 1942
Lithograph on paper
LSU Museum of Art, 68.9.20
Gift of the Artist

Opposite:
CAROLINE WOGAN DURIEUX
Bipeds Dancing, 1932
Lithograph on paper
LSU Museum of Art, 68.9.3
Gift of the Artist

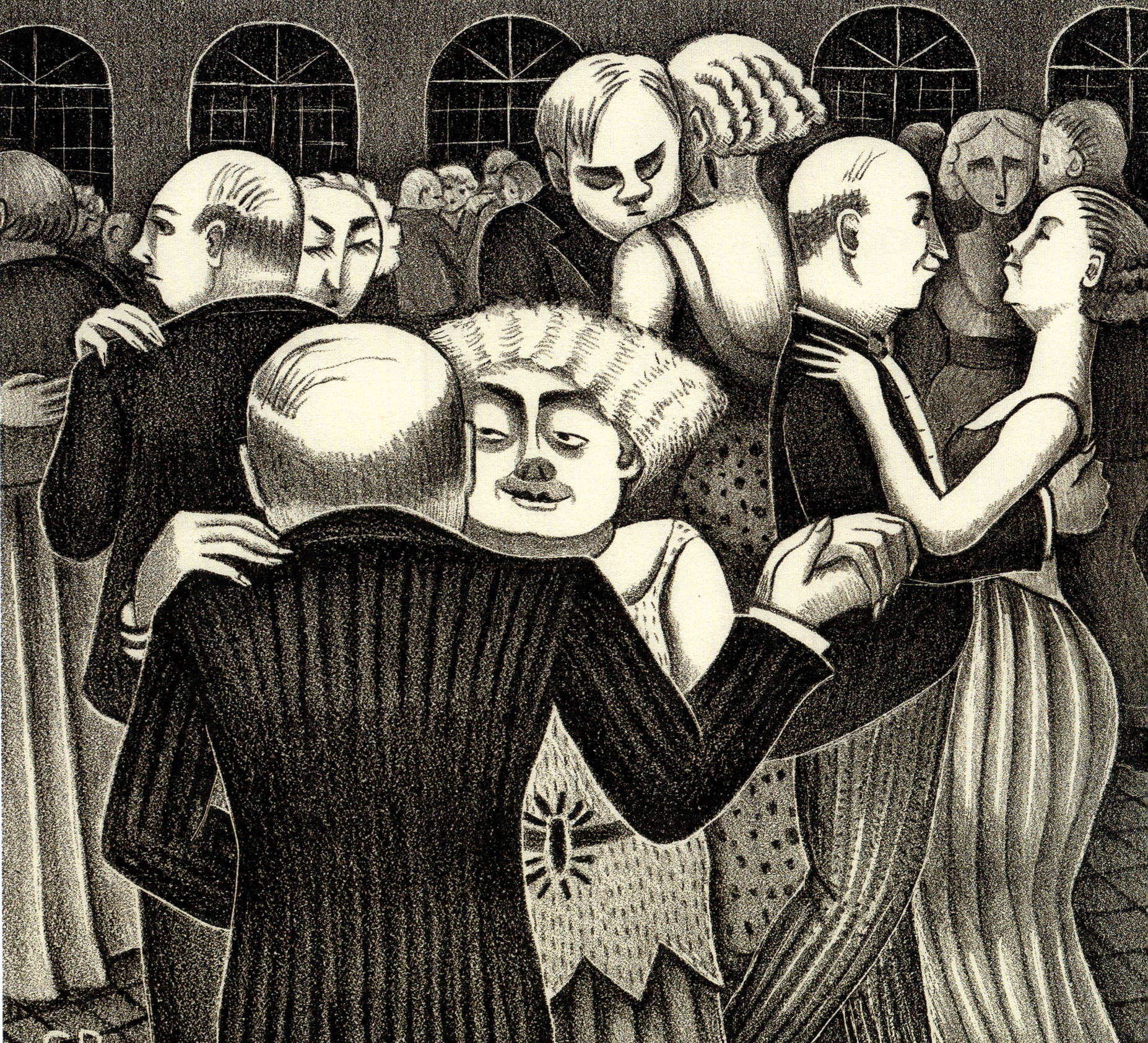

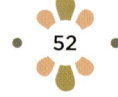

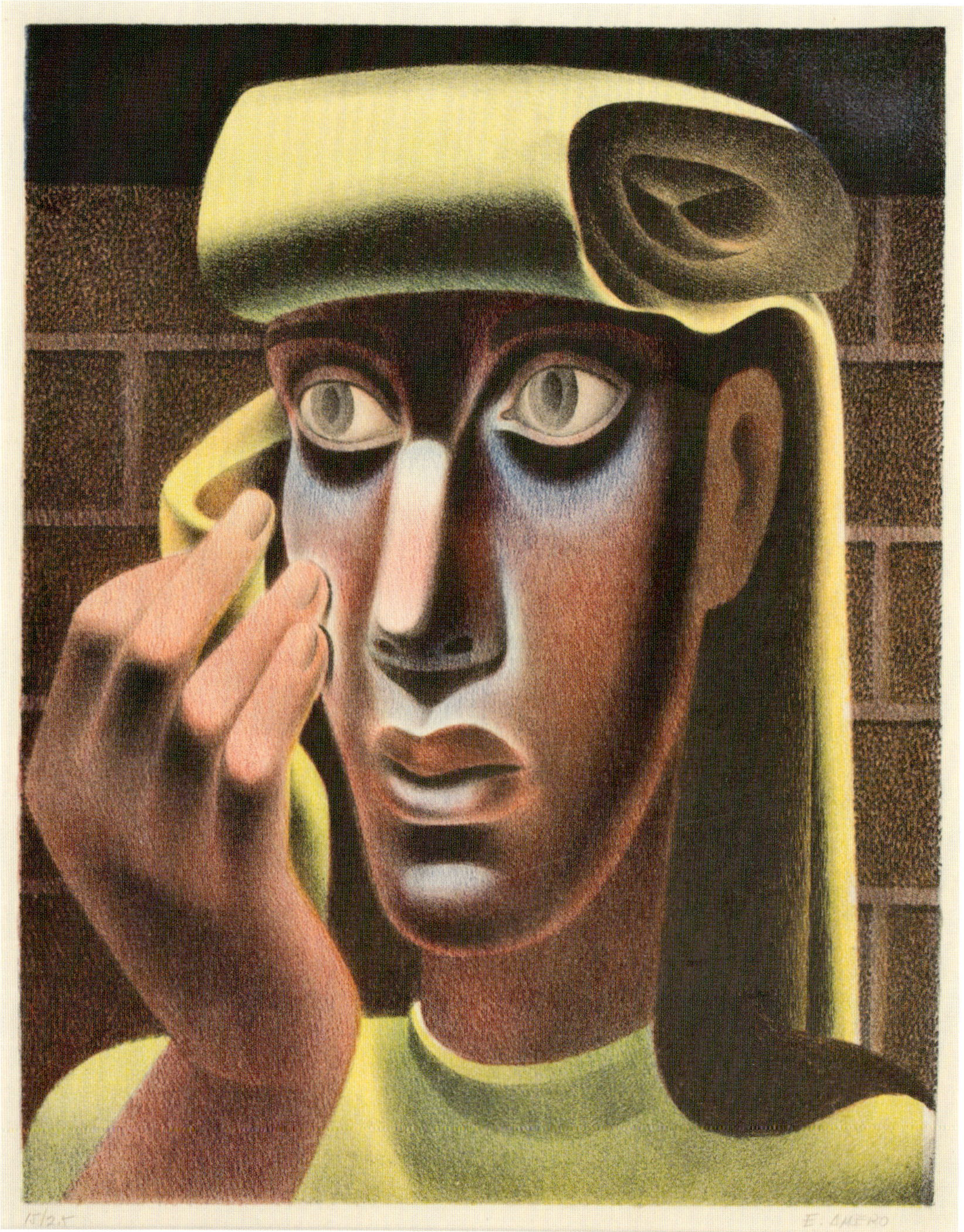

EMILIO AMERO
The Gesture (El Gesto), 1948
Lithograph on paper
Meadows Museum of Art
Stein Collection of Don Brown Works

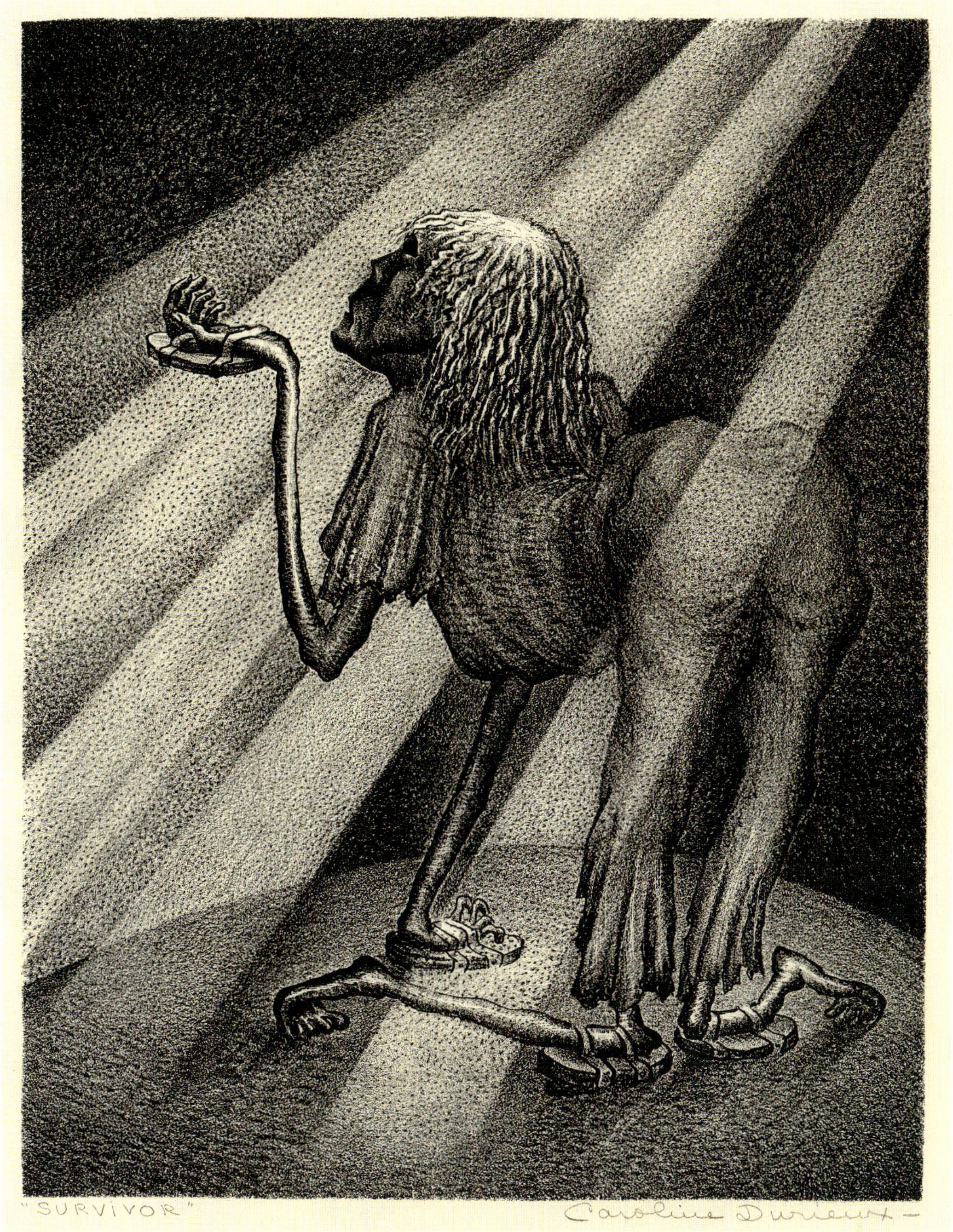

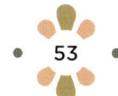

Caroline Wogan Durieux
Survivor, 1947
Black and white lithograph on paper
LSU Museum of Art, 68.9.48
Gift of the Artist

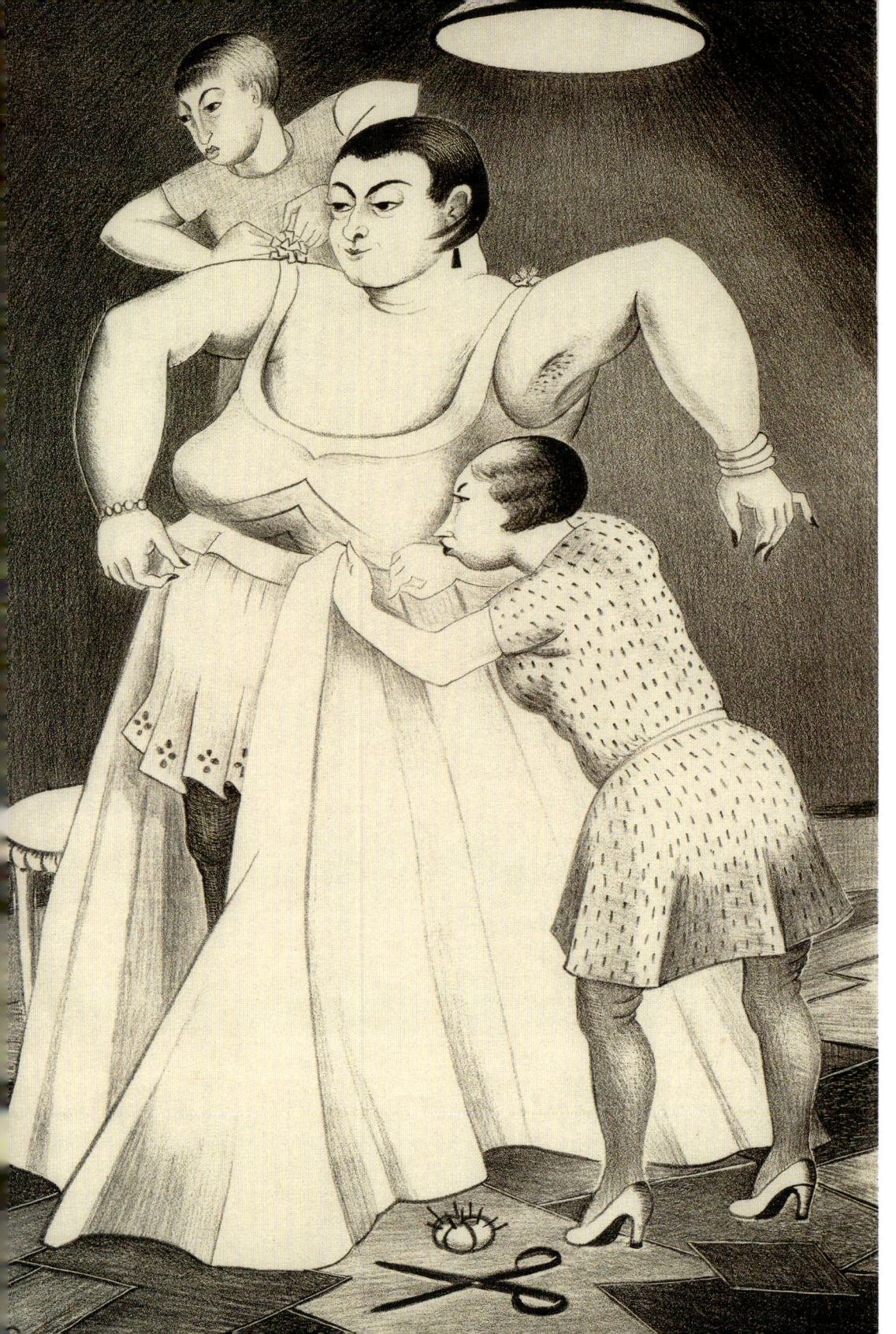

Caroline Wogan Durieux
Dressmaking, 1932
Lithograph on paper
LSU Museum of Art, 68.9.4
Gift of the Artist

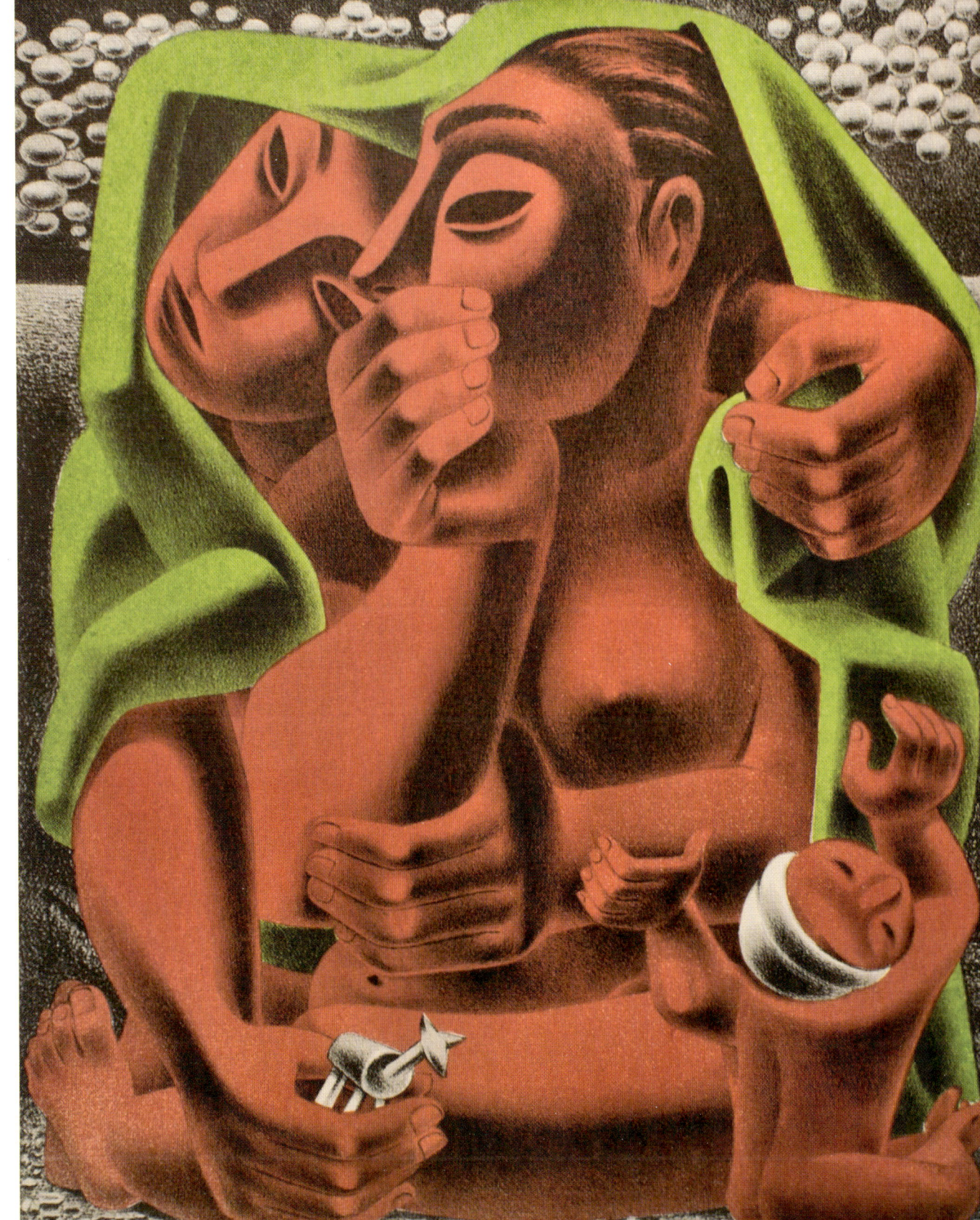

EMILIO AMERO
Where? Donde?, 1929-1950
Color lithographic ink on warm white rag paper
Meadows Museum of Art
Stein Collection of Don Brown Works

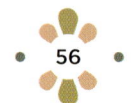

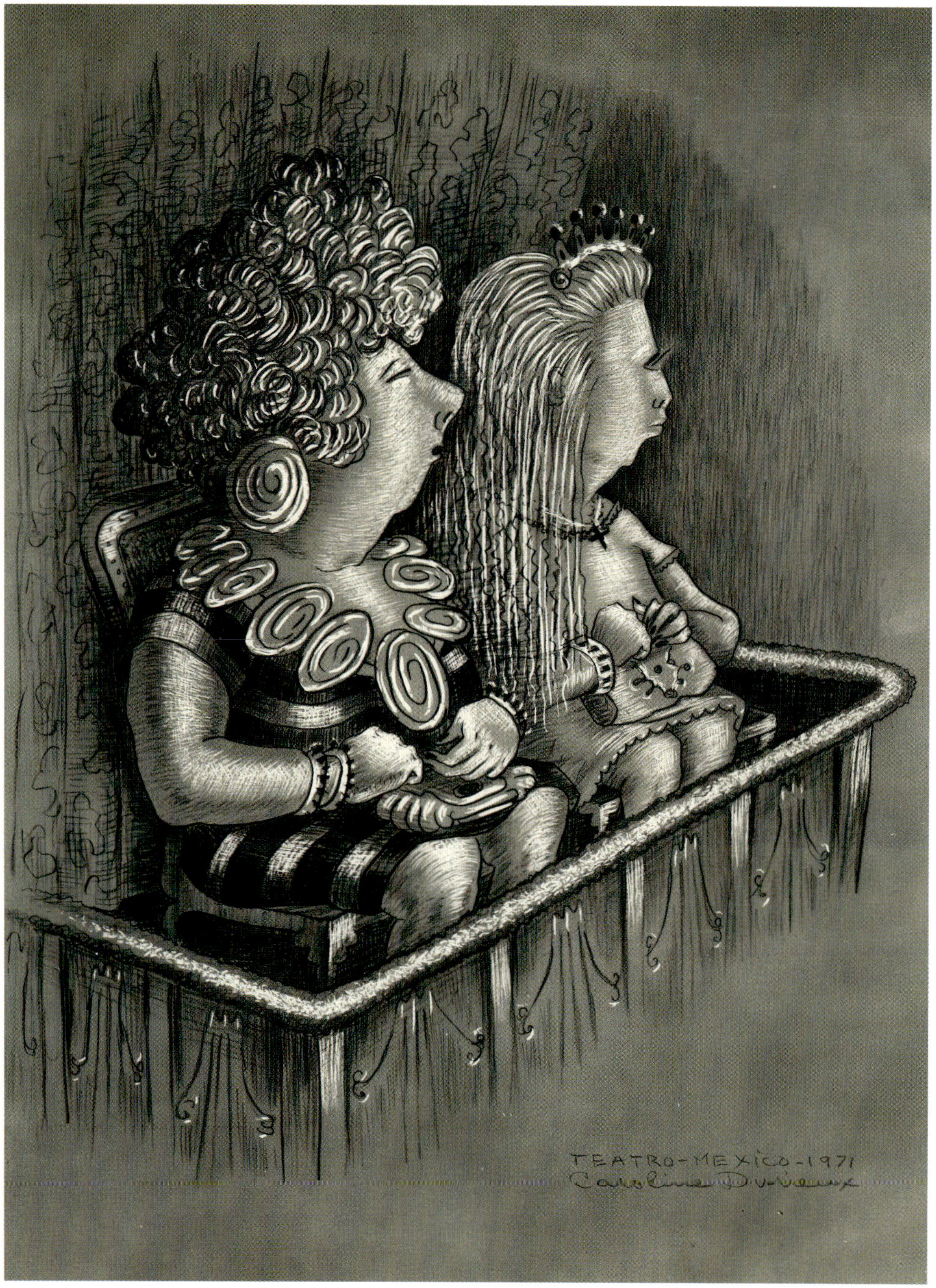

CAROLINE WOGAN DURIEUX
Teatro, 1971
Black and white cliché verre
LSU Museum of Art, 76.12.2
Gift of Caroline Durieux and Mrs. Frank Woody

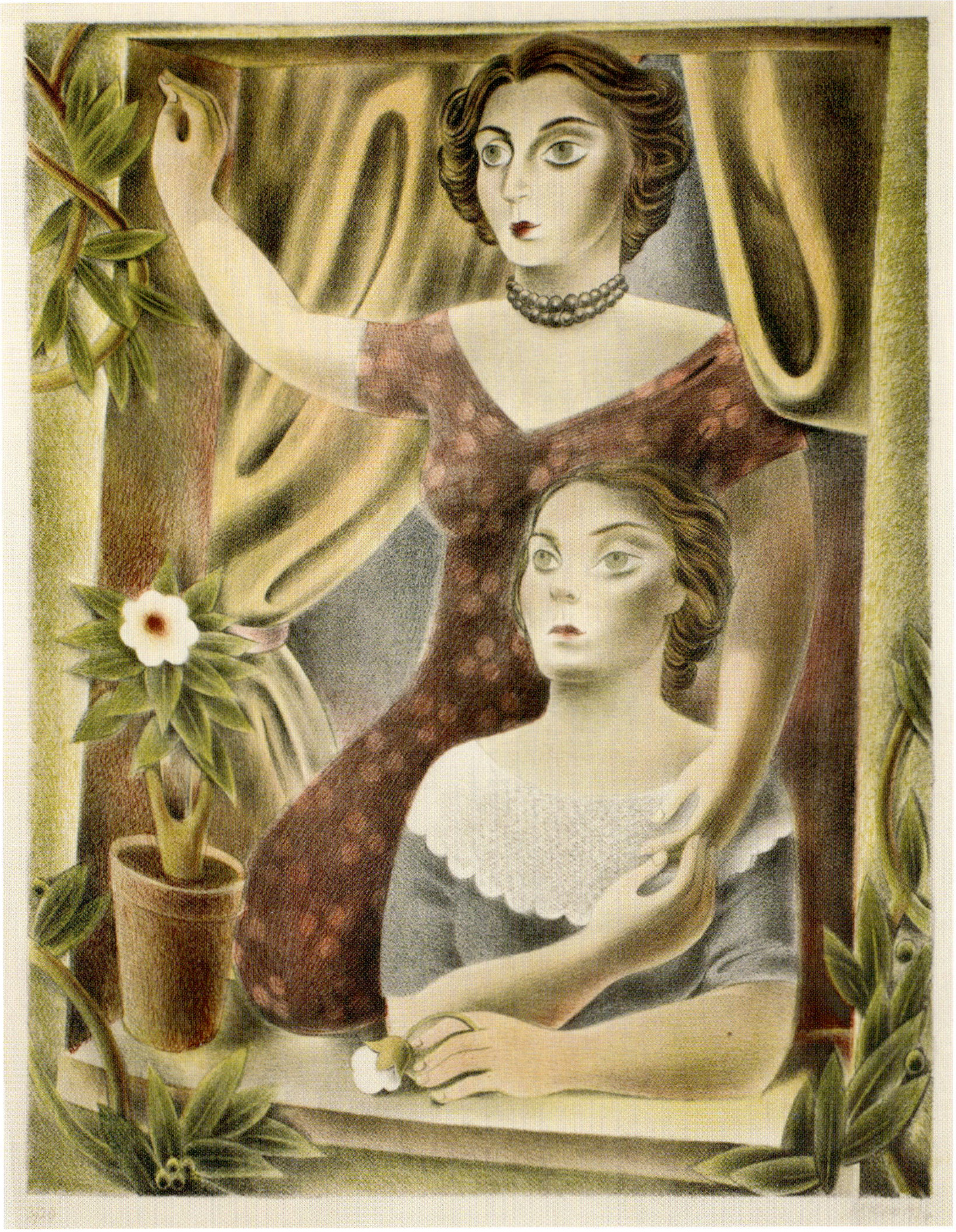

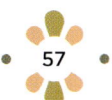

57

EMILIO AMERO
The Florence Cane Daughters (Las Hijas de Florence Cane), 1936
Lithograph in red, green, yellow, blue and black on cream woven paper
Meadows Museum of Art
Stein Collection of Don Brown Works

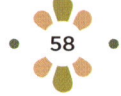

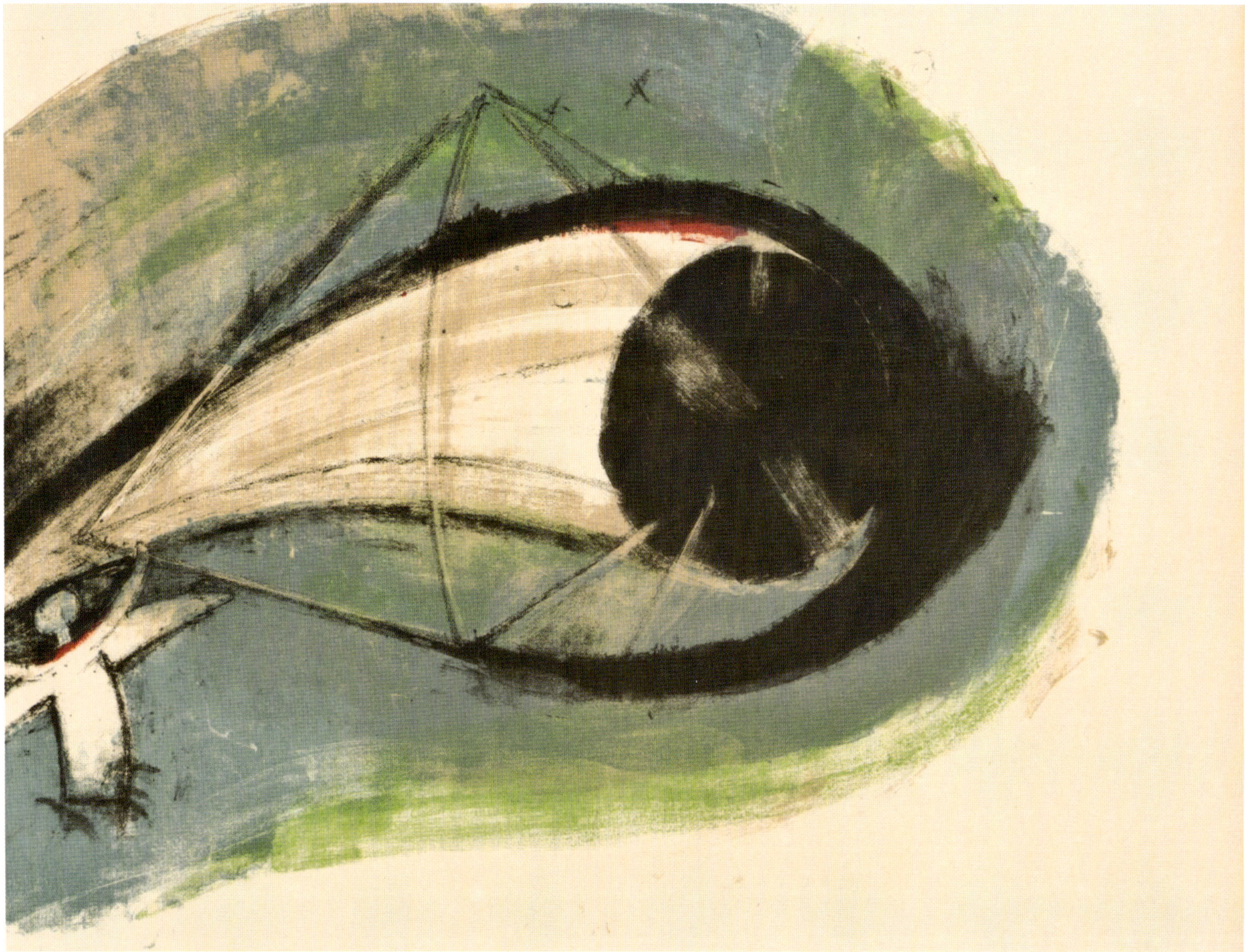

Rufino Tamayo
Illustrations from the Apocalypse de Saint, 1959
Color lithographic ink on warm, handmade paper
Meadows Museum of Art

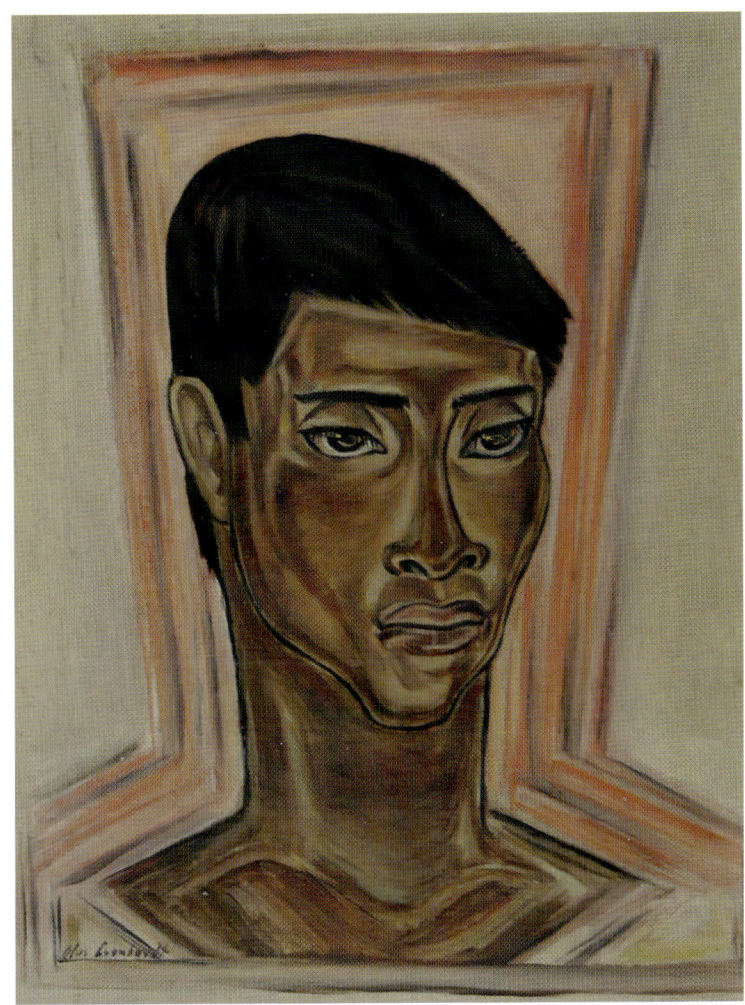

OLIVE LEONHARDT
Above: *Oaxaca Boy,* c. 1930s and Right: *Orizaba Man,* c. 1930s
Oil on board
Collection of Gay Leonhardt

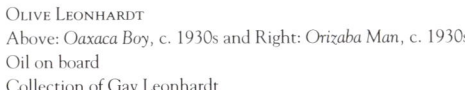

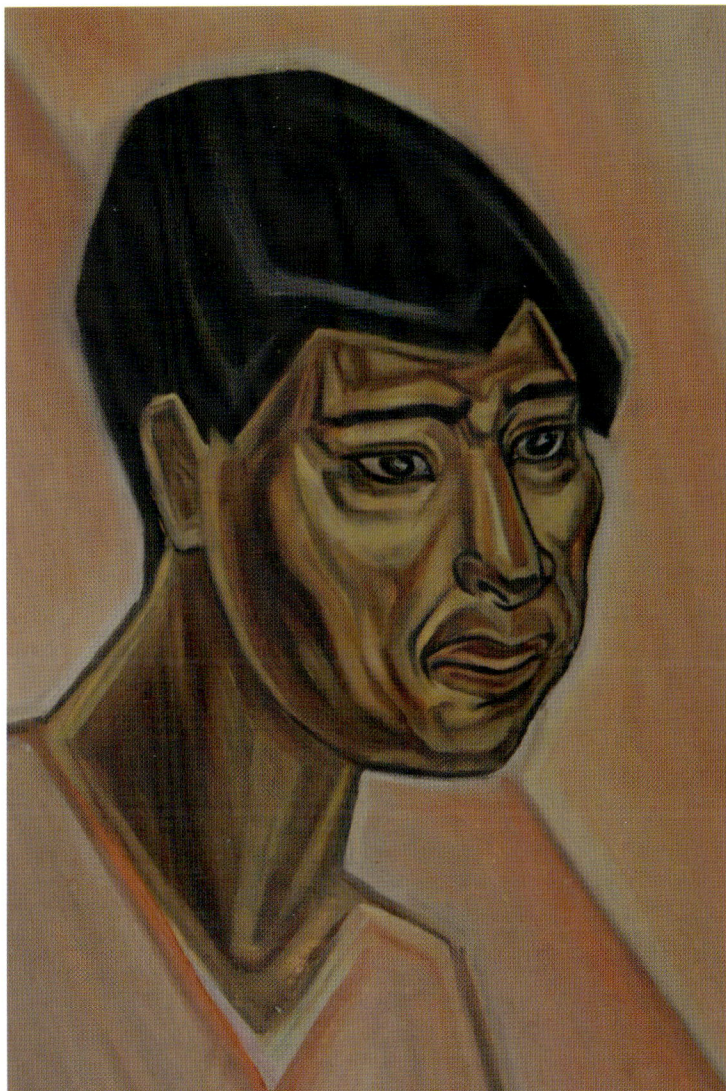

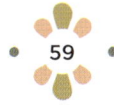

Olive Leonhardt shared a studio with Caroline Durieux in New Orleans in the 1920s and, like Durieux, travelled to Mexico in the 1930s. Leonhardt's time in Mexico proved formative for her artistic development, and while living in Mexico she created a striking series of oil paintings, sketches, and drawings of Mexican subjects and scenes. In a 1931 interview with a New Orleans journalist, she asserted that the more politically minded art she encountered in Mexico was a necessary response to times of great social and political upheaval.

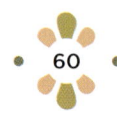

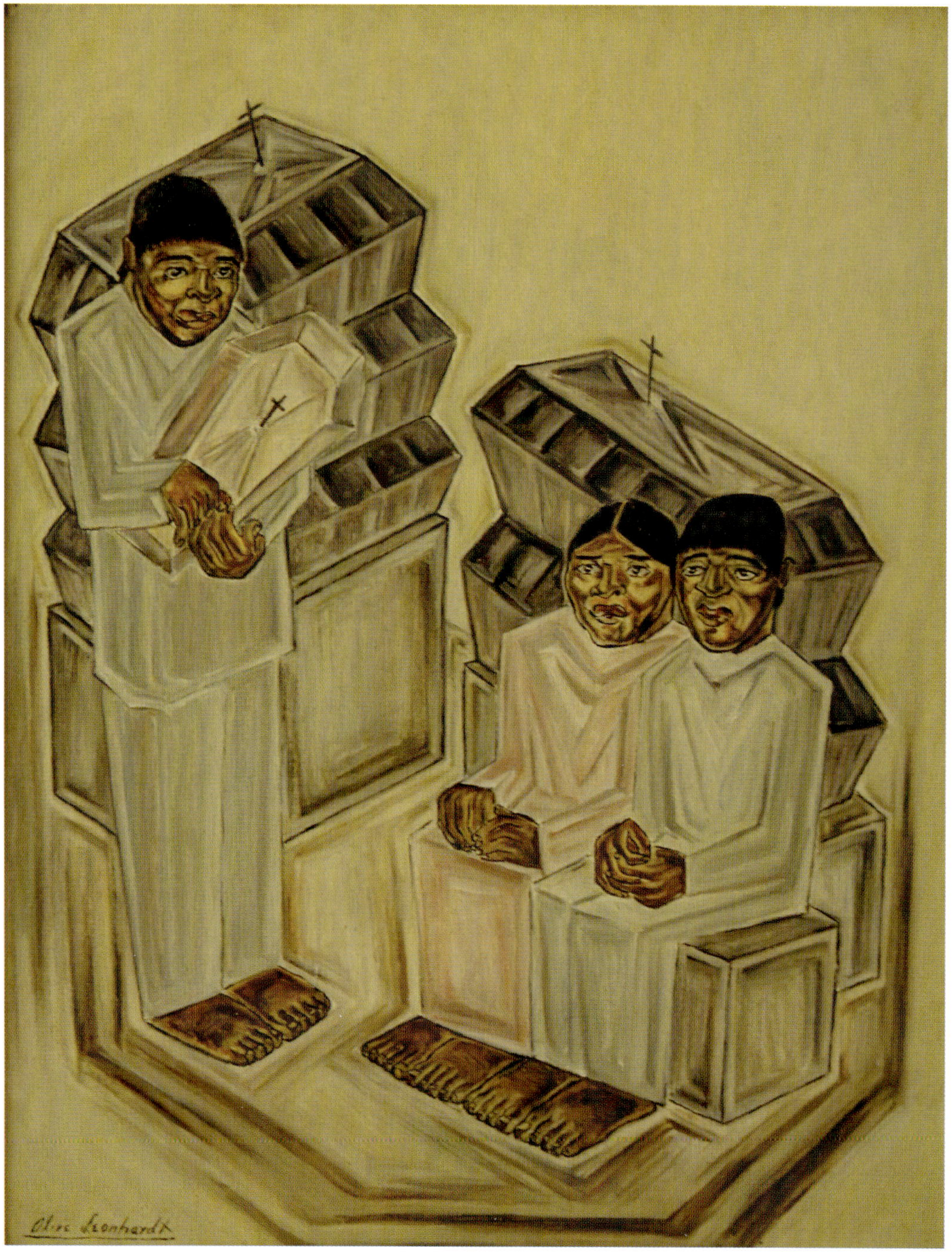

Olive Leonhardt
Shopping, c. 1935-39
Oil on board
Collection of Gay Leonhardt

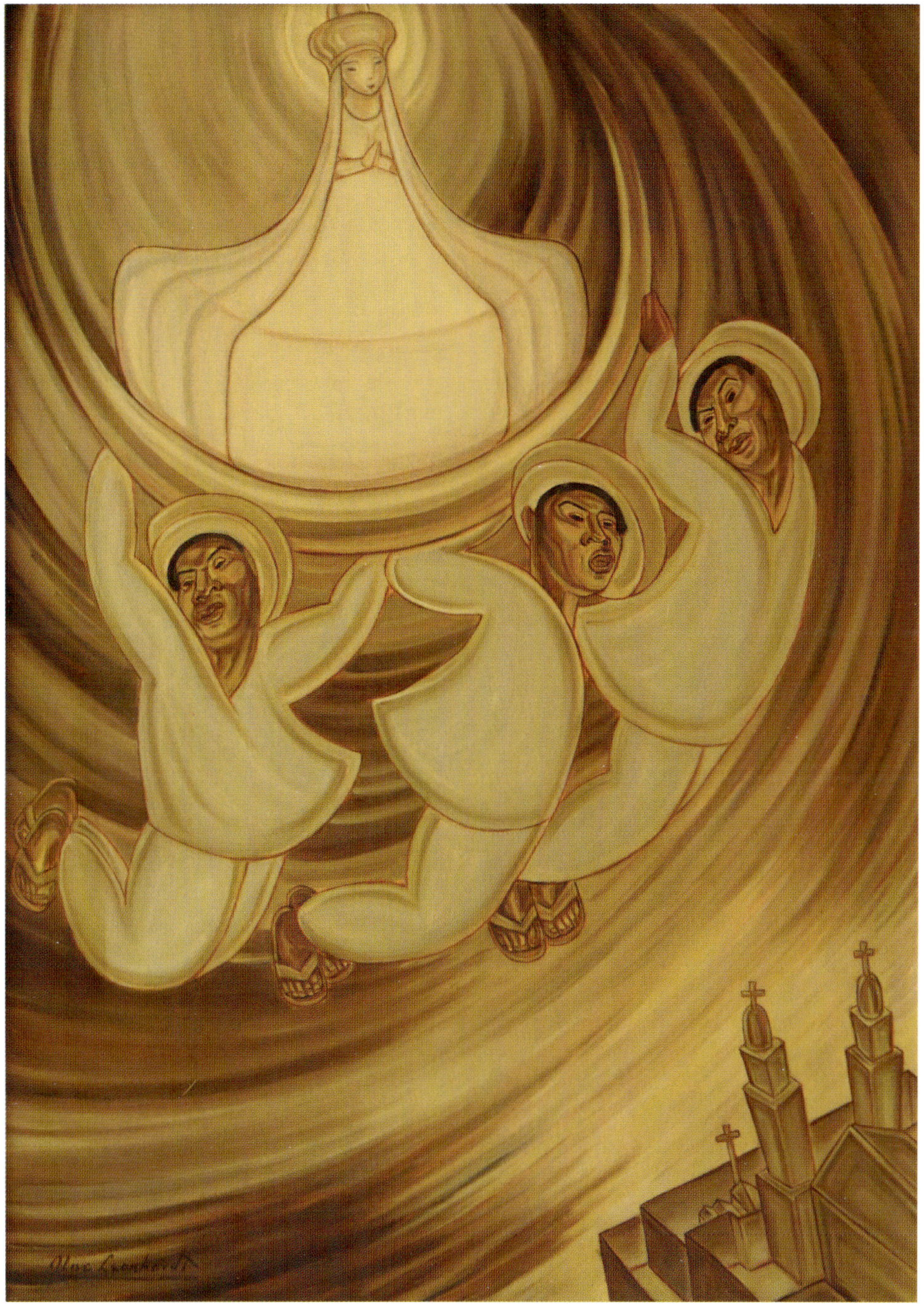

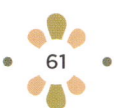

OLIVE LEONHARDT
Blessed Virgin Returns to the Fiesta, c. 1935-39
Oil on canvas
Collection of Gay Leonhardt

61

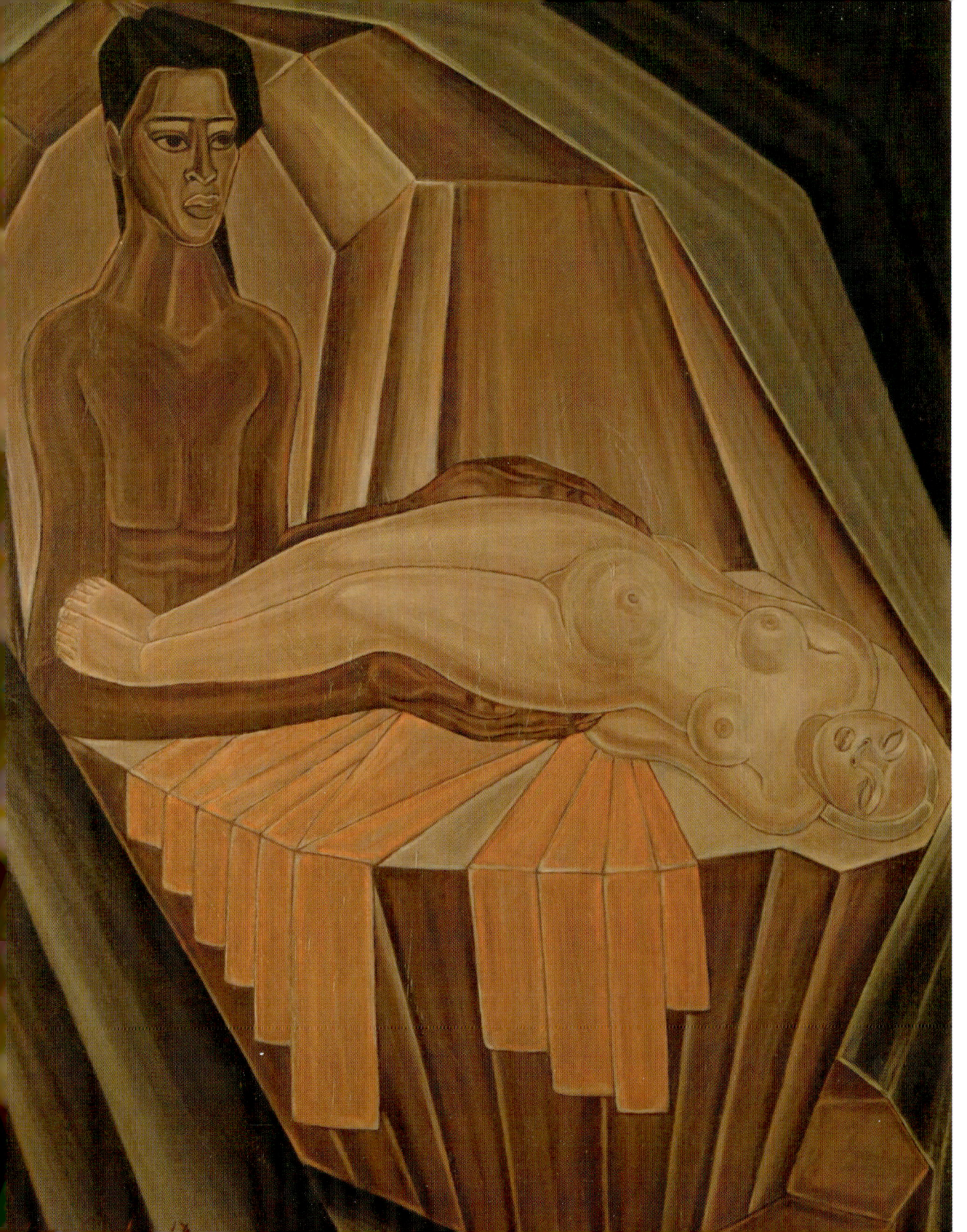

OLIVE LEONHARDT
The Tomb, c. 1935-39
Oil on canvas
Collection of Gay Leonhardt

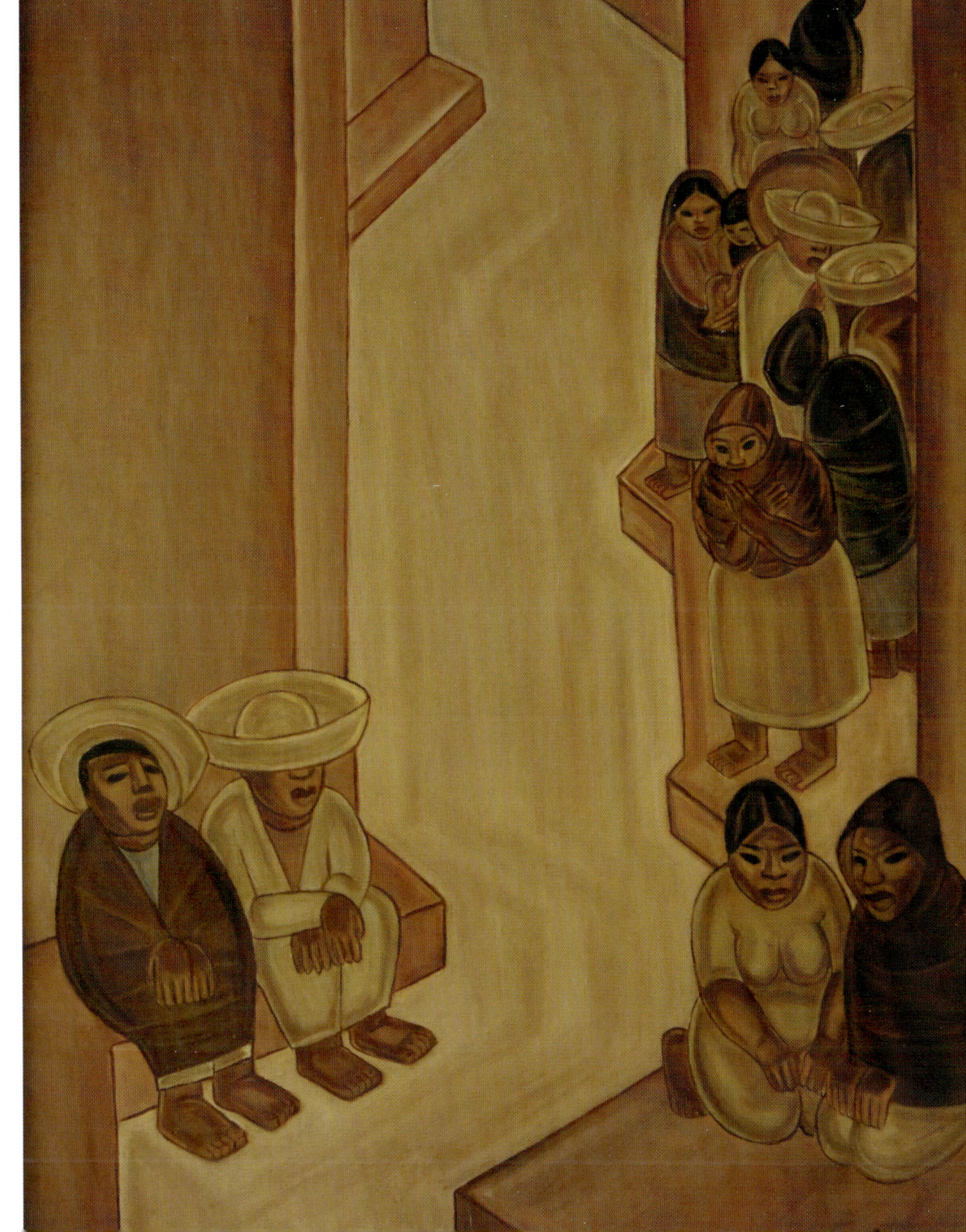

Olive Leonhardt
Calla Manana, c. 1935-39
Oil on canvas
Collection of Gay Leonhardt

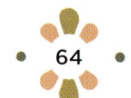

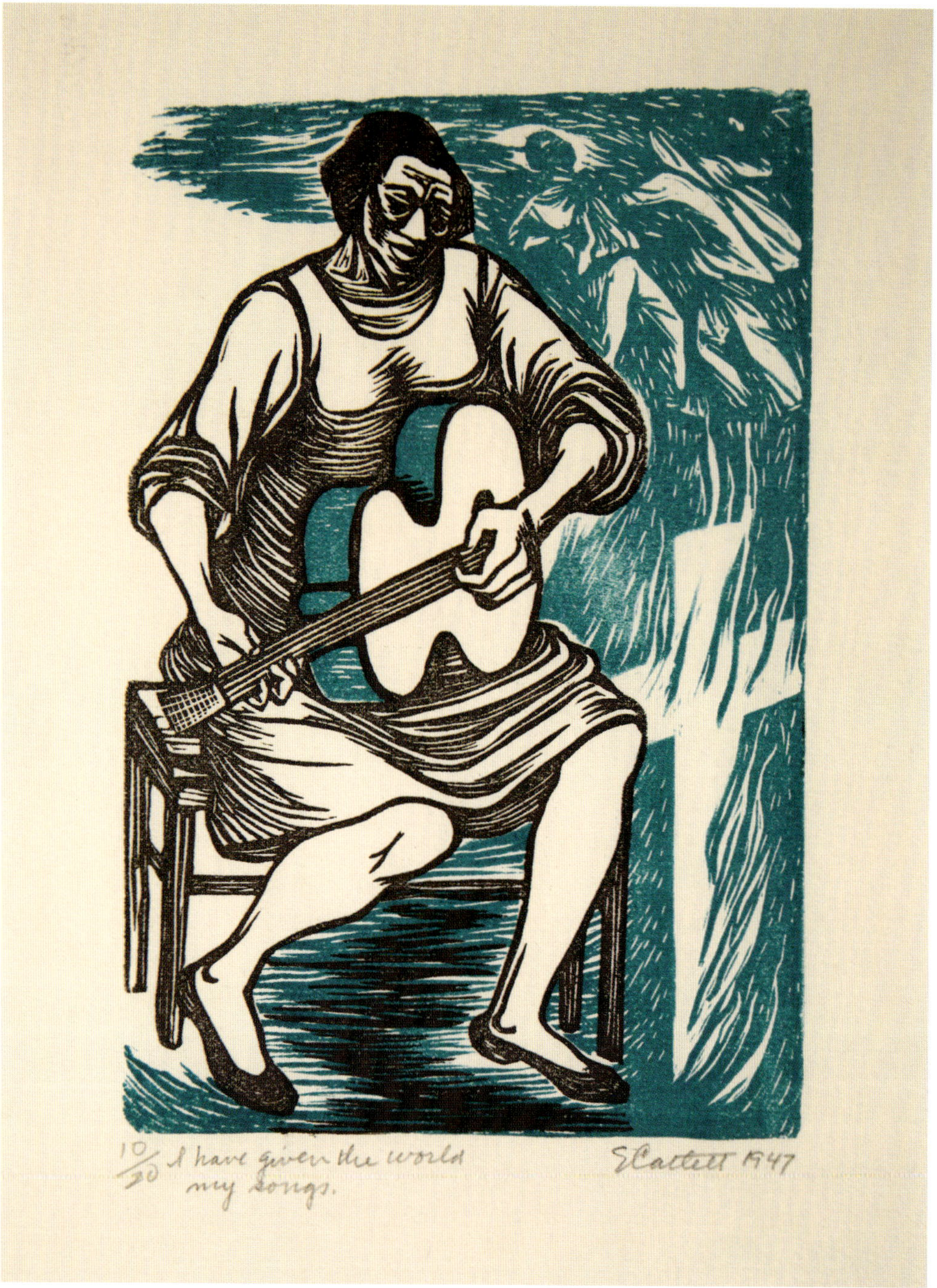

10/30 *I have given the world my songs.* ℰCatlett 1947

ELIZABETH CATLETT
I have given the world my songs, 1947 (printed 1989)
Linocut
The Historic New Orleans Collection, 2013.0222.5
Acquisition made possible by the Laussat Society

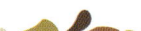

African-American sculptor and printmaker Elizabeth Catlett taught at Dilliard University in New Orleans in the 1940s and was made an honorary citizen of the city for her influential sculptures and prints depicting African-American life in the South. Catlett received an art fellowship to study in Mexico in 1946 and remained in Mexico for the rest of her life, becoming an influential teacher at the famed Mexico City printmaking collective Taller de Gráphica Popular. Catlett created her *The Negro Woman* series, which chronicles the experiences of African-American women in the United States, while living and working in Mexico. Catlett saw clear corollaries between the political conditions in Mexico and the lives of African-Americans in the United States, viewing both countries as part of a shared struggle for liberation and freedom.

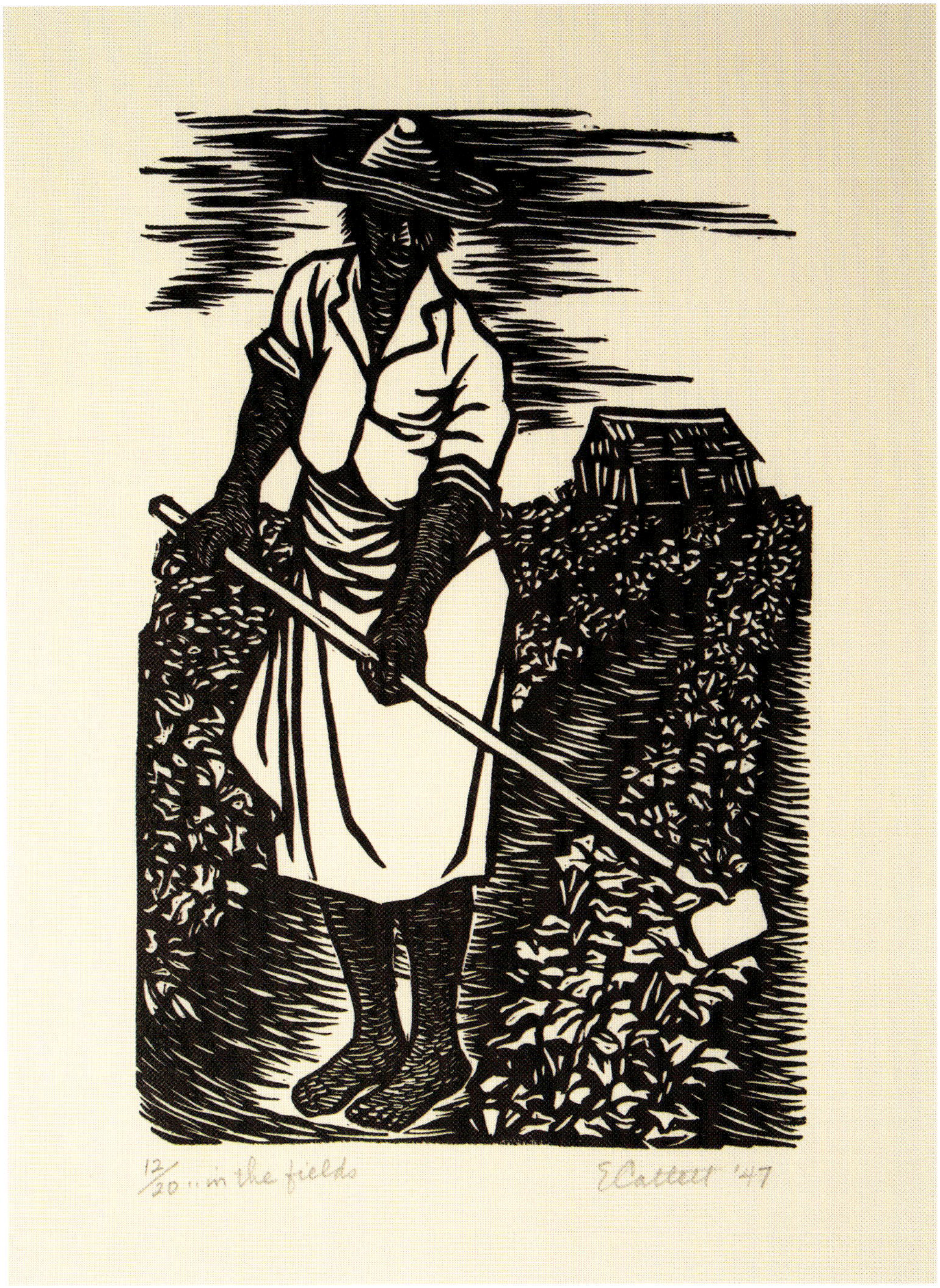

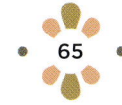

ELIZABETH CATLETT
...In the Fields, 1947 (printed 1989)
Linocut
The Historic New Orleans Collection, 2013.0222.3
Acquisition made possible by the Laussat Society

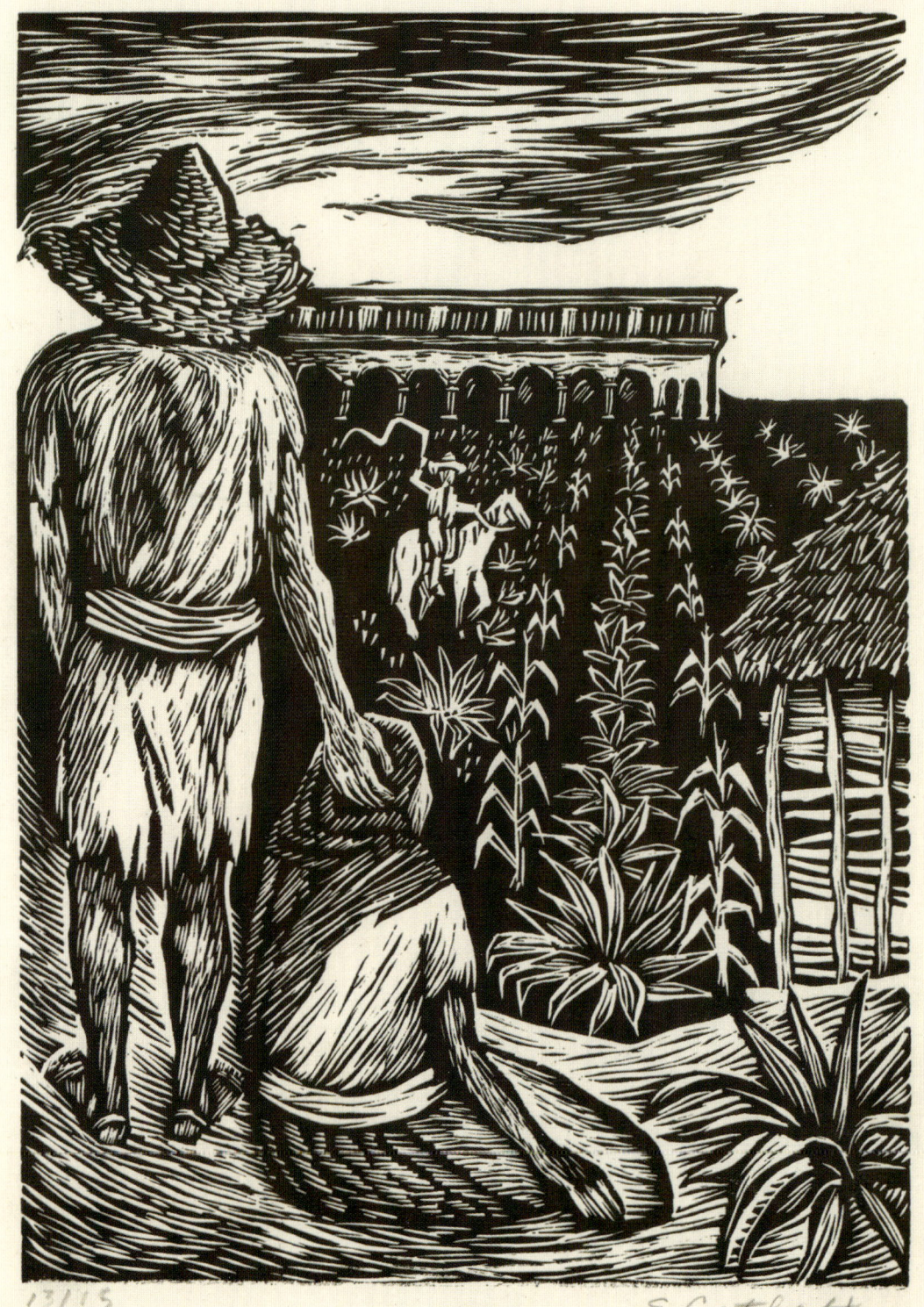

13/15   E Catlett

ELIZABETH CATLETT
Peones Mexicano, 1945 and 47
Linocut
The Historic New Orleans Collection, 2014.0077.5

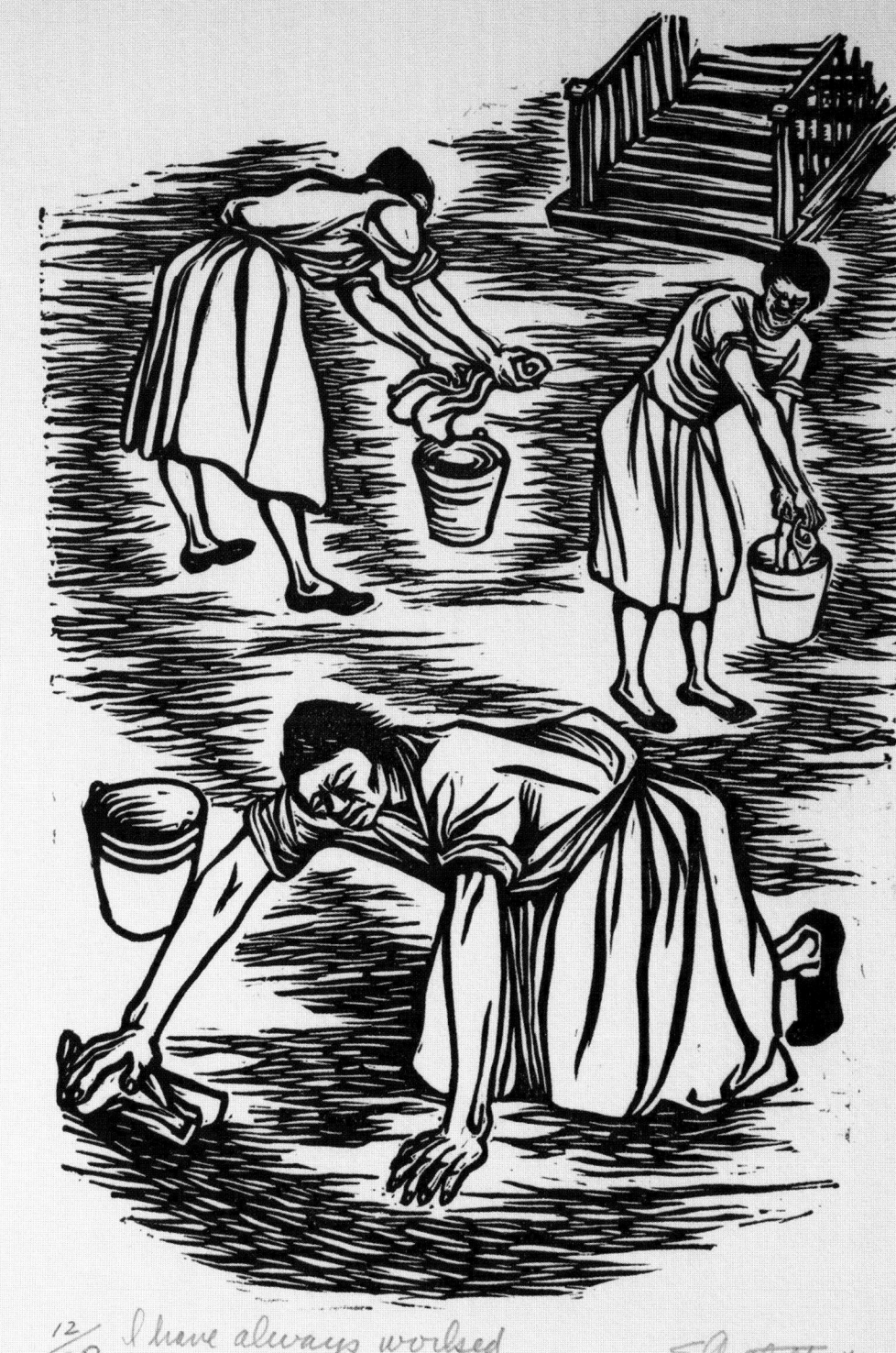

Elizabeth Catlett
I have always worked hard in America, 1946 (printed 1989)
Linocut
The Historic New Orleans Collection, 2013.0222.2
Acquisition made possible by the Laussat Society

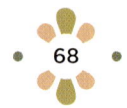

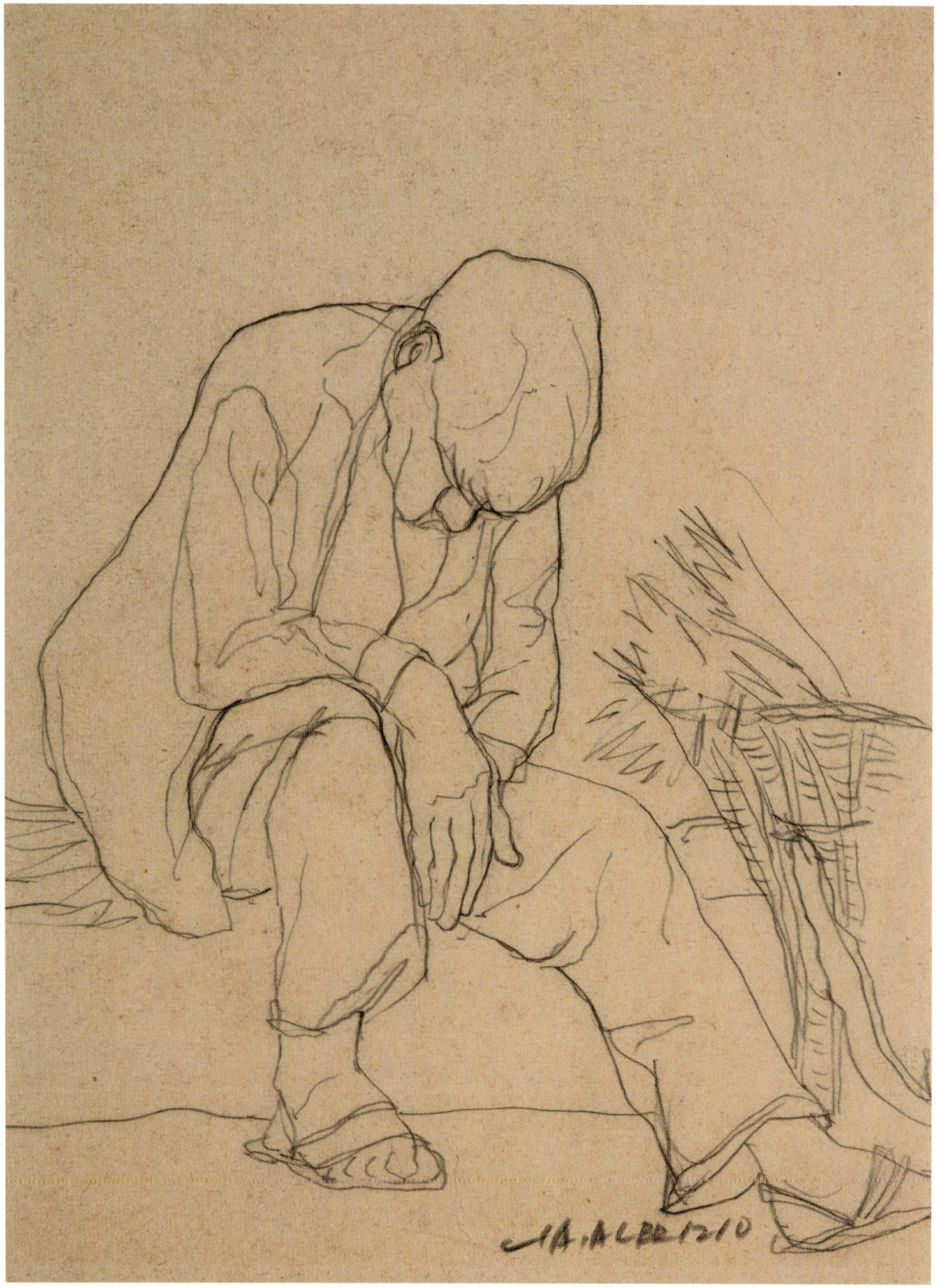

Conrad A. Albrizio
Seated Mexican Peasant, 1947
Pencil on paper
LSU Museum of Art, 93.17.3
Gift of Dr. and Mrs. Robert B. Smythe

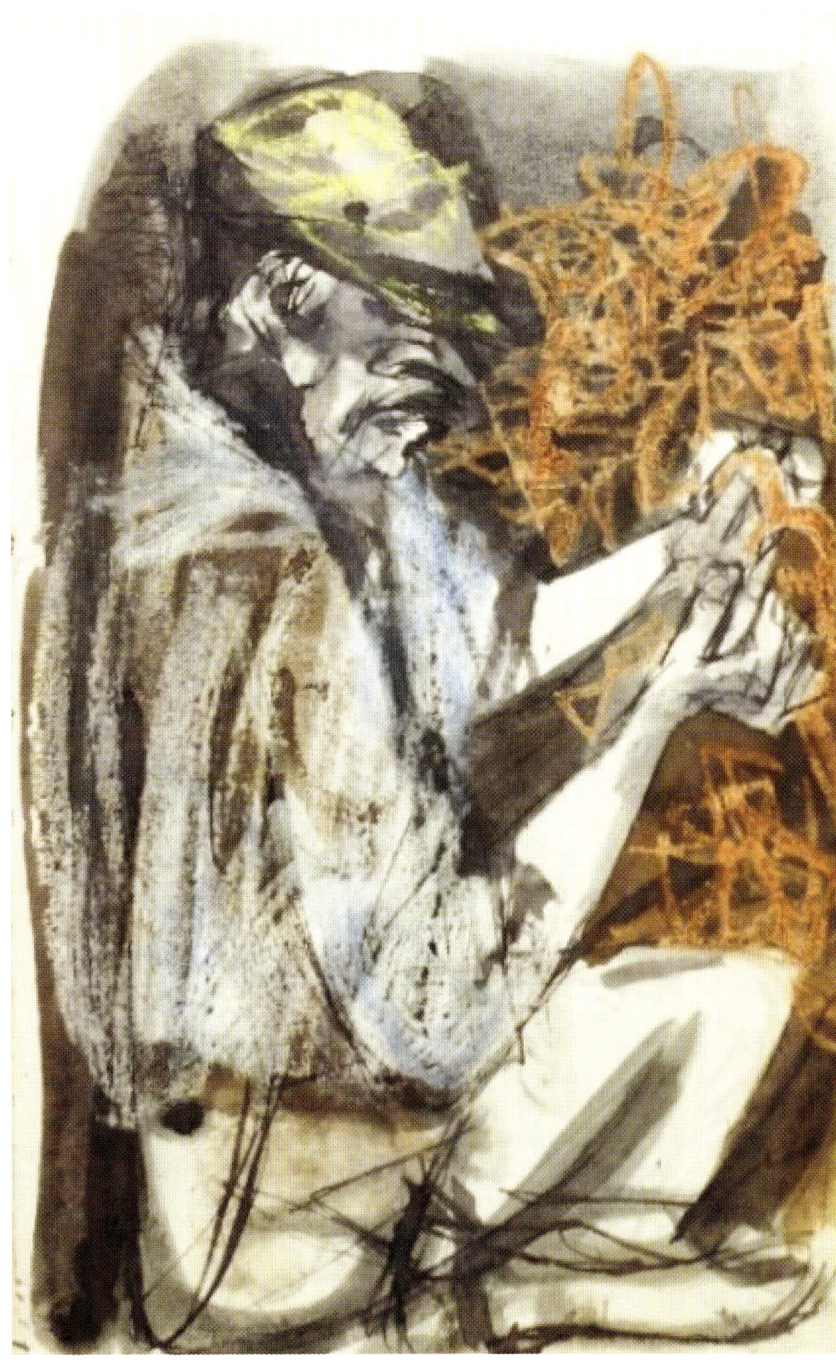

Edward Millman
Bayou-Nutria Series, c. 1940s
Lithograph on paper
LSU Museum of Art
Gift of Mark and Catherine K. Potter and the Paula G. Manship Museum of Art
Endowment for Acquisition and Conservation

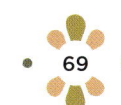

69

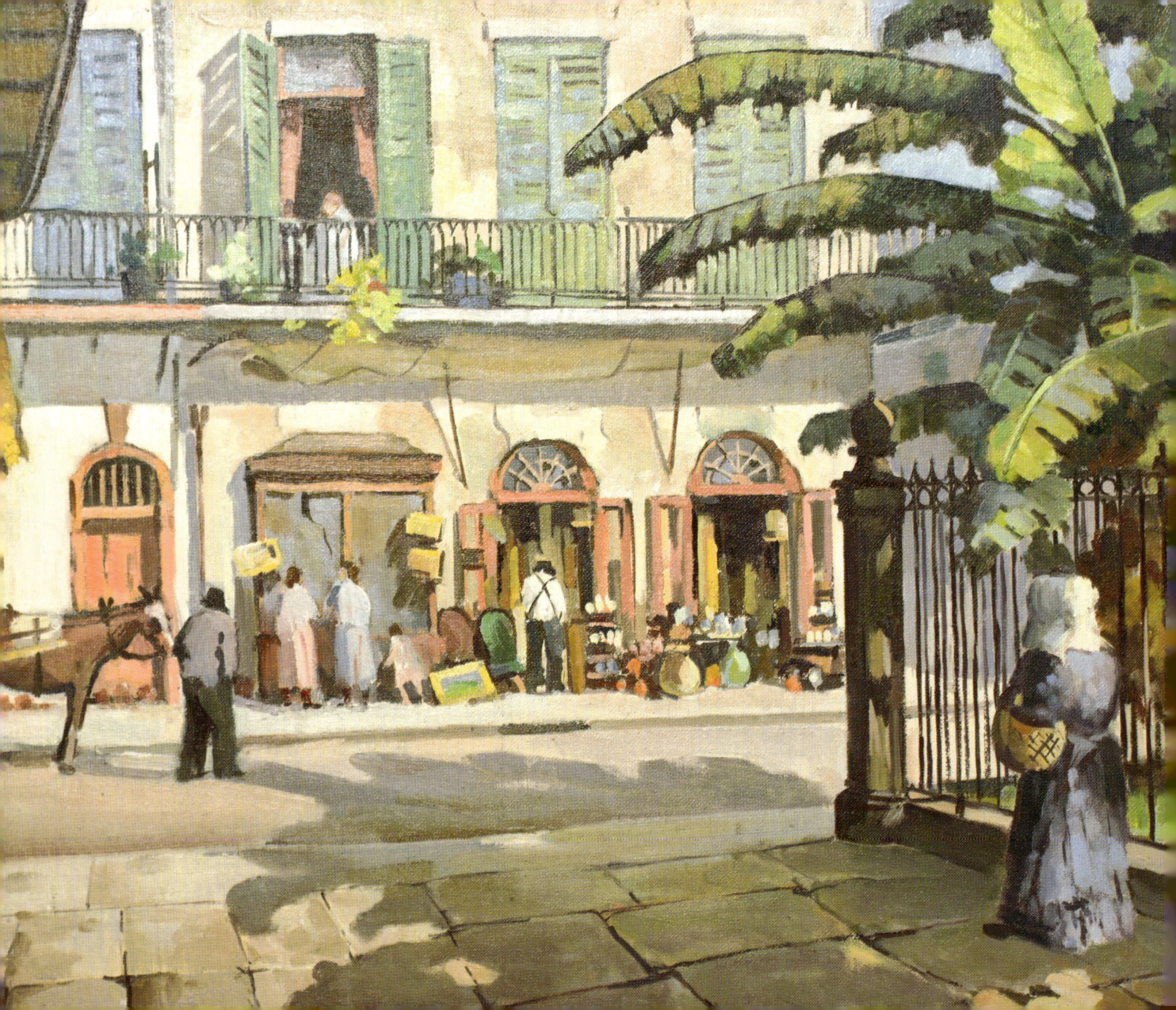

Opposite:
CLARENCE MILLET
French Quarter Scene, c. 1930
Oil on canvas
LSU Museum of Art, 2006.7.10
Gift of the Friends of LSU Libraries
Transfer from LSU Libraries' Special Collections

Right:
MORRIS HENRY HOBBS
Calle de Guadalupe, Taxco, Mexico, 1942
Etching on paper
LSU Museum of Art, MOA 10.205.23
Gift of Dr. A. Brooks Cronan, Jr. and Diana Cronan

The lush and romantic images of New Orleans made by Louisiana artists like Boyd Cruise, Clarence Millet, and Morris Henry Hobbs often portrayed the city as an exotic locale more closely tied to South America and Europe than the rest of the United States. All three of these Louisiana artists also travelled to Mexico and produced similarly exotic Mexican scenes that reinforced the shared allure of both locales. During this period, several exhibitions at the New Orleans Arts and Crafts Club emphasized New Orleans' Mexican connections by displaying Mexican and New Orleanian scenes side-by-side. In a 1927 review of just such an exhibition at the New Orleans Arts and Crafts Club, *The Times Picayune* commented on the strong visual similarities between the two places, noting that the images of Mexico and of Louisiana on view at the exhibition were "held together by a considerable unity," and characterizing both the Mexican and Louisianan images as "Southern scenes," whether they originated in "the United States or in its neighbor Mexico."

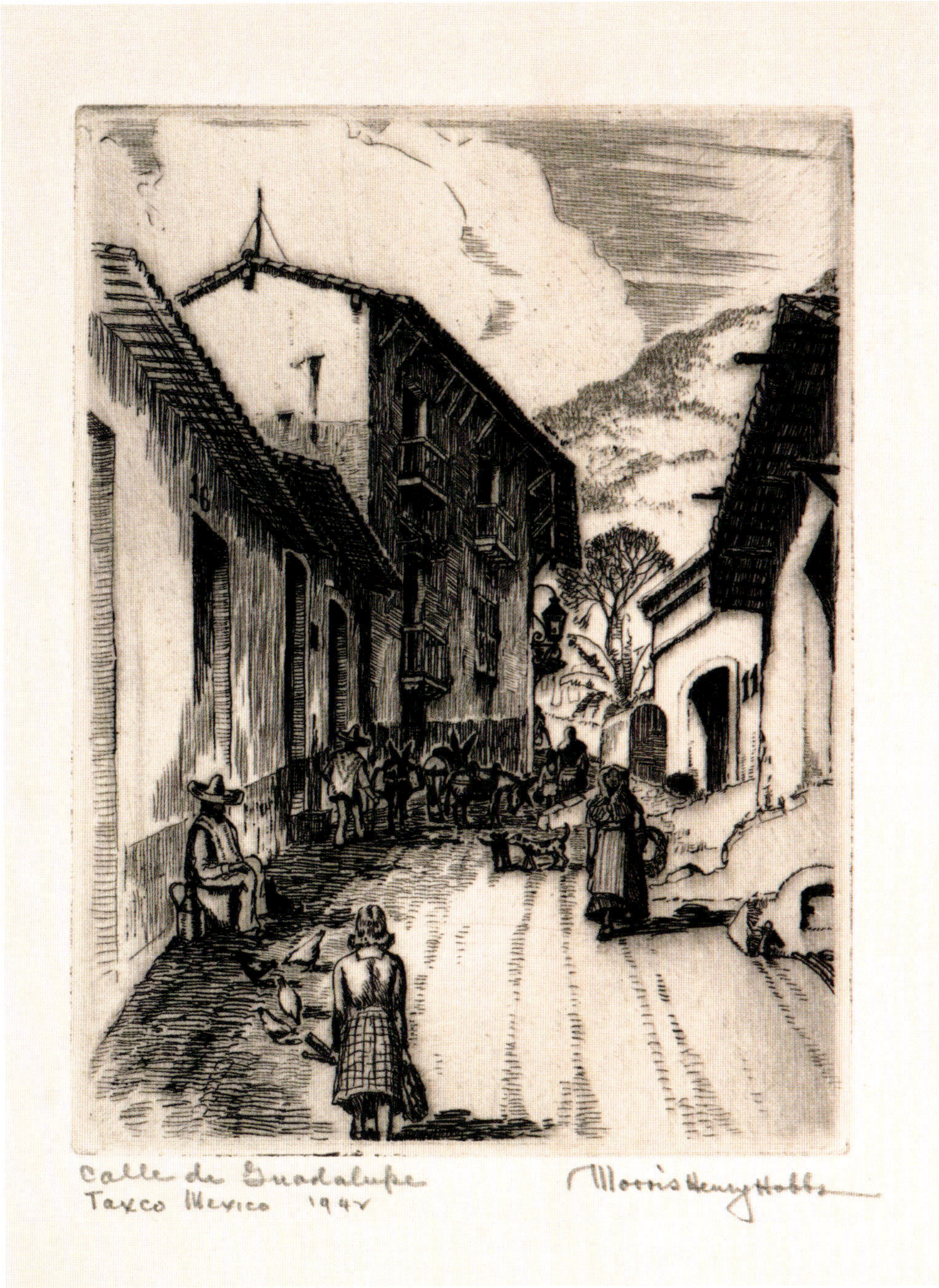

Calle de Guadalupe
Taxco Mexico 1942

Morris Henry Hobbs

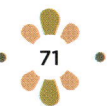

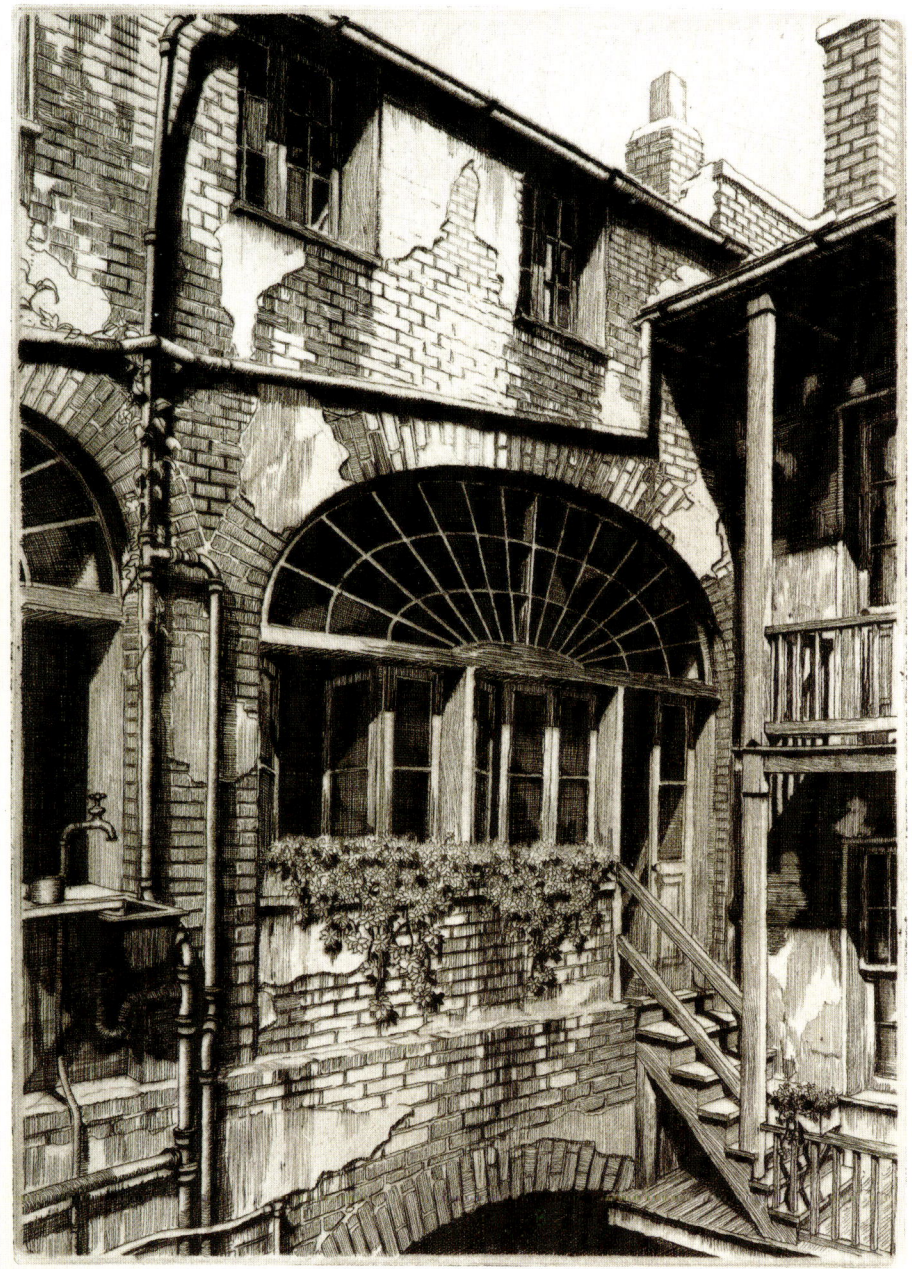

Old Fan Window
New Orleans

Morris Henry Hobbs

Morris Henry Hobbs
Old Fan Window, New Orleans, u.d.
Etching on paper
Private Collection
Photo © David Humphreys, 2015

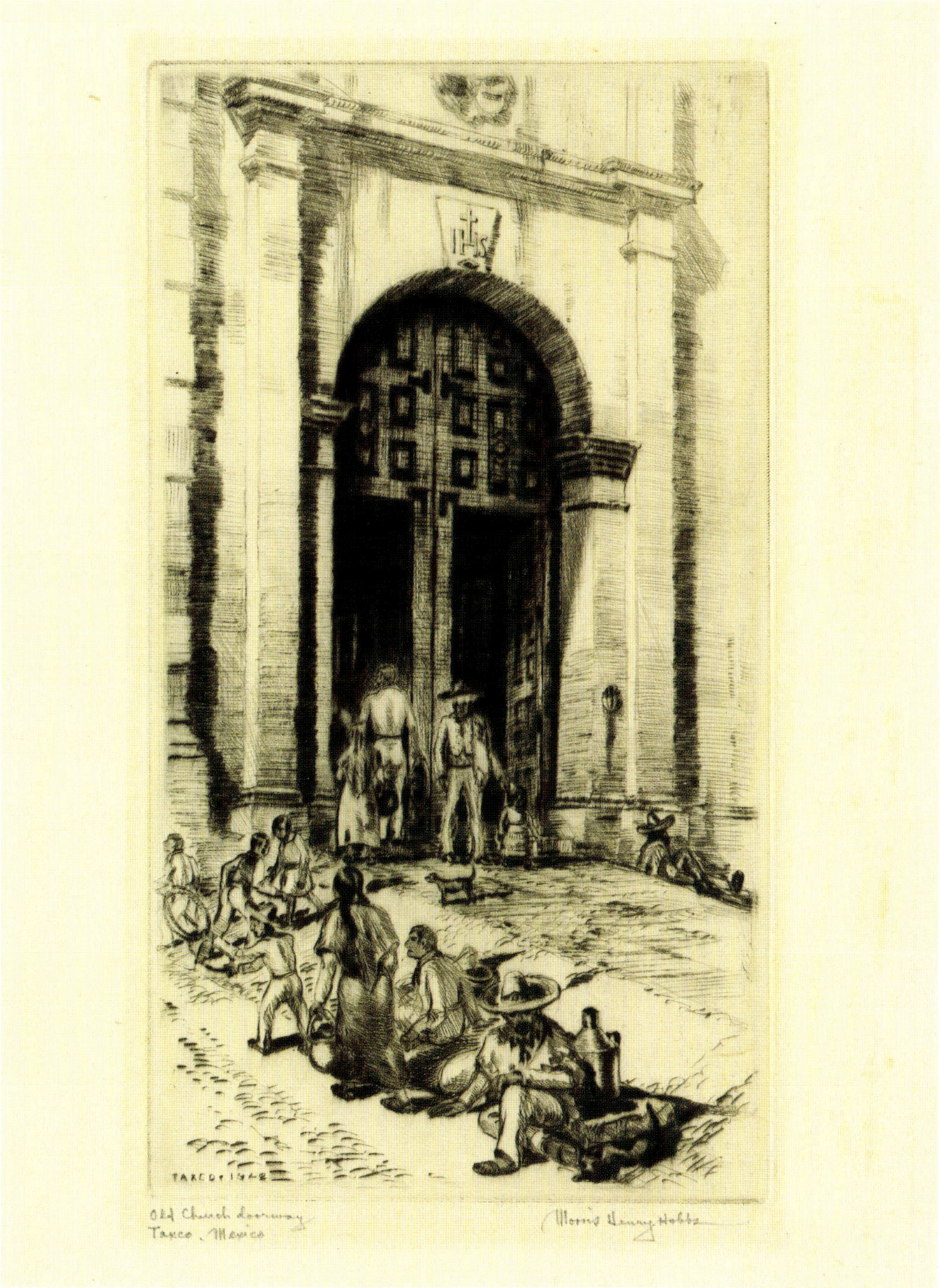

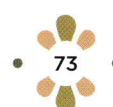

73

MORRIS HENRY HOBBS
Old Church Doorway Taxco, Mexico, 1942
Drypoint etching on paper
The Latin American Library, Tulane University
Reed Isbell Collection of Morris Henry Hobbs Etchings of Mexico

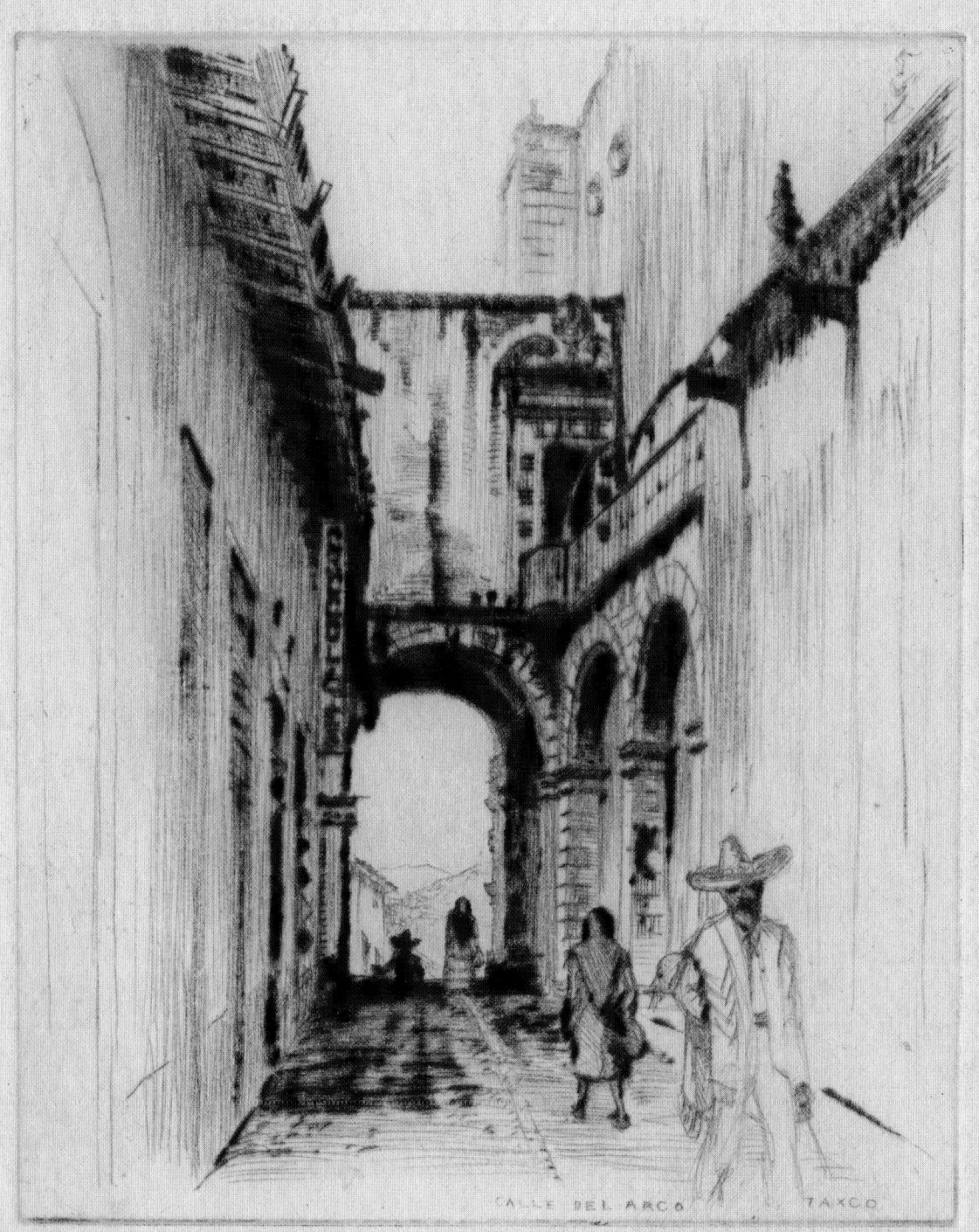

CALLE DEL ARCO — TAXCO

Morris Henry Hobbs
Calle de Arco, u.d.
Etching on paper
The Latin American Library, Tulane University
Reed Isbell Collection of Morris Henry Hobbs Etchings of Mexico

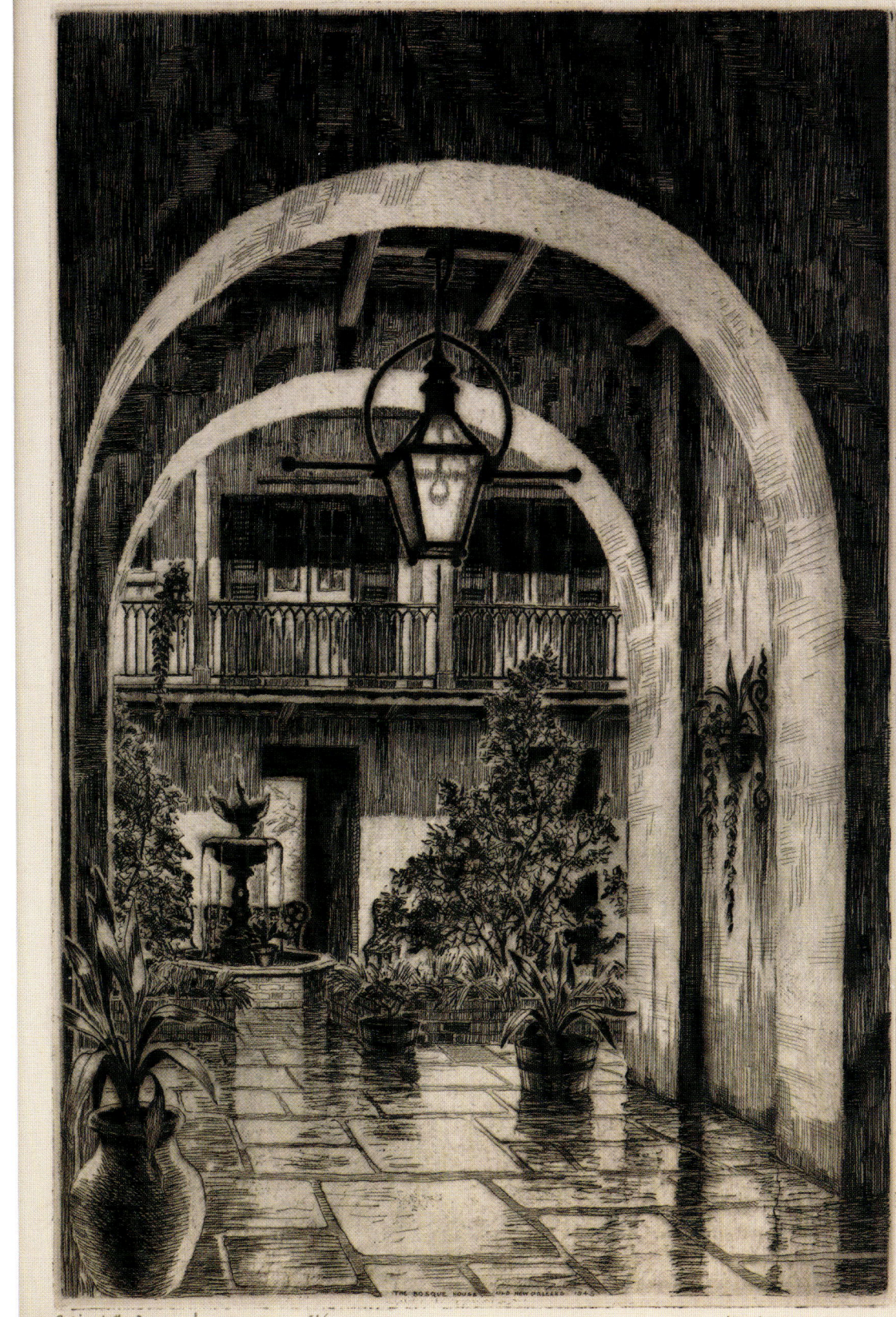

Morris Henry Hobbs
Patio of the Bosque House, Old New Orleans, 1945
Etching on Paper
Private Collection
Photo © David Humphreys, 2015

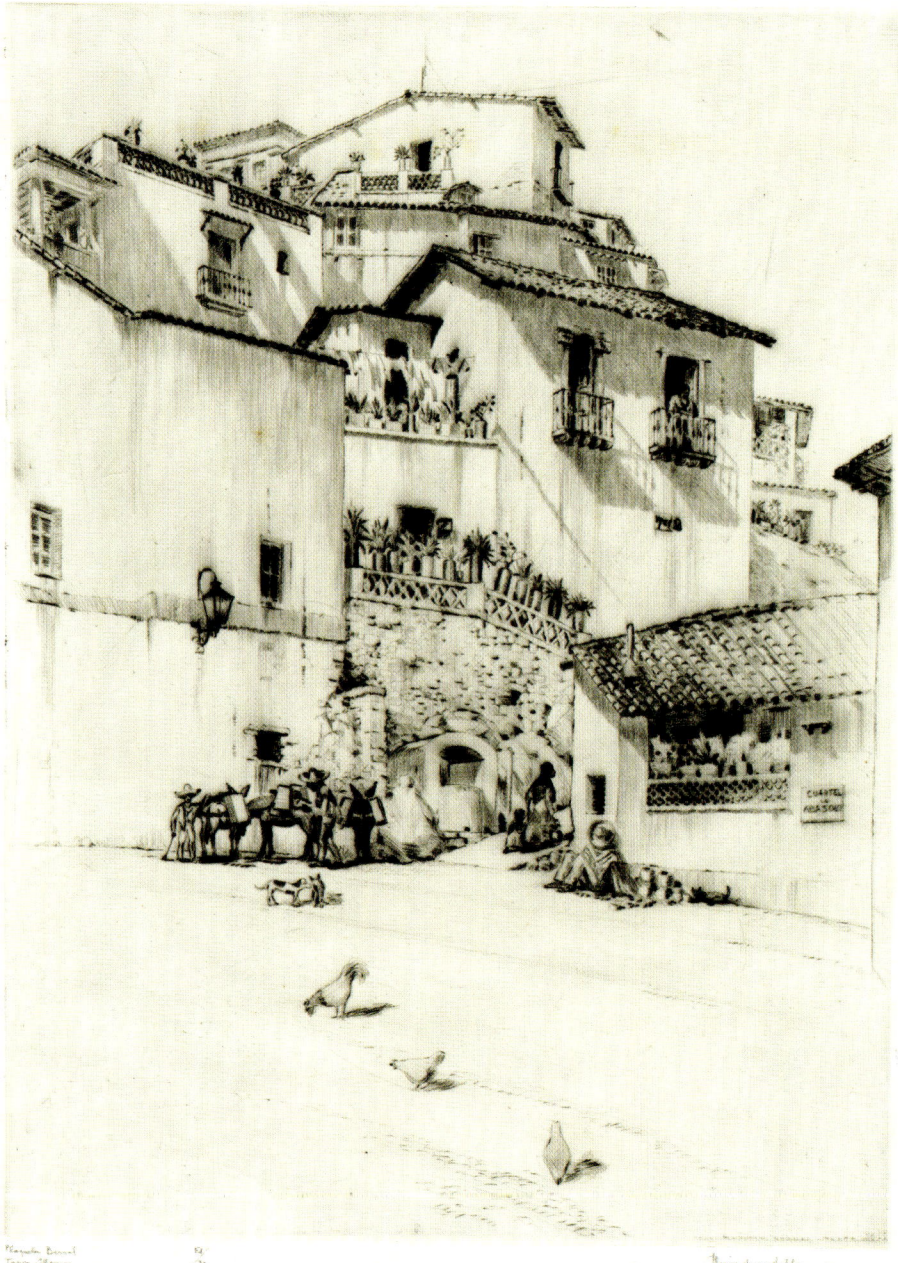

Left:
Morris Henry Hobbs
Plazuela Bernal, Taxco, Mexico, 1942
Drypoint etching on paper
The Latin American Library, Tulane University
Reed Isbell Collection of Morris Henry Hobbs Etchings of Mexico

Opposite:
Morris Henry Hobbs
Iron Lace, 1949
Etching on paper
Private Collection
Photo © David Humphreys, 2015

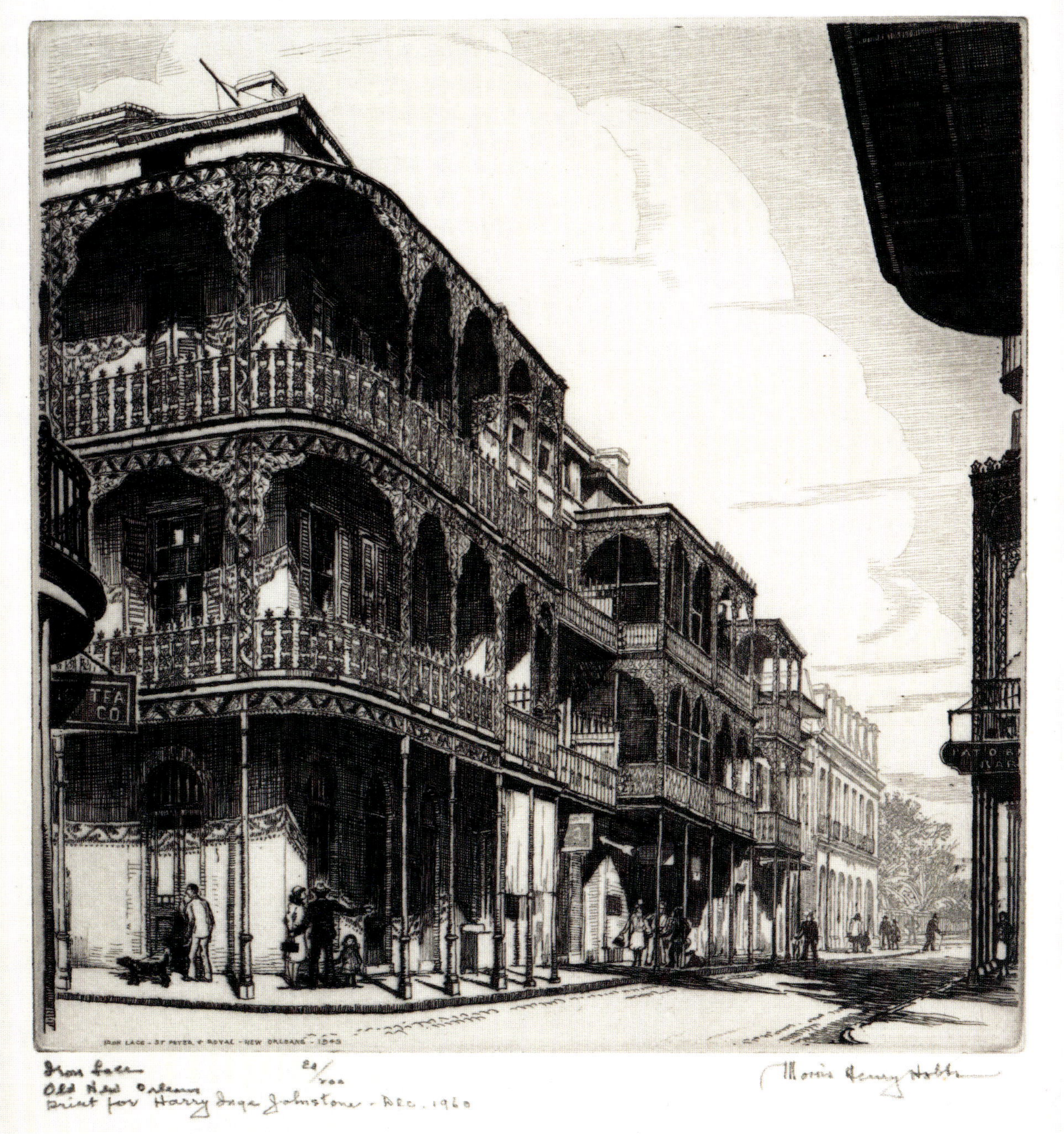

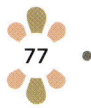

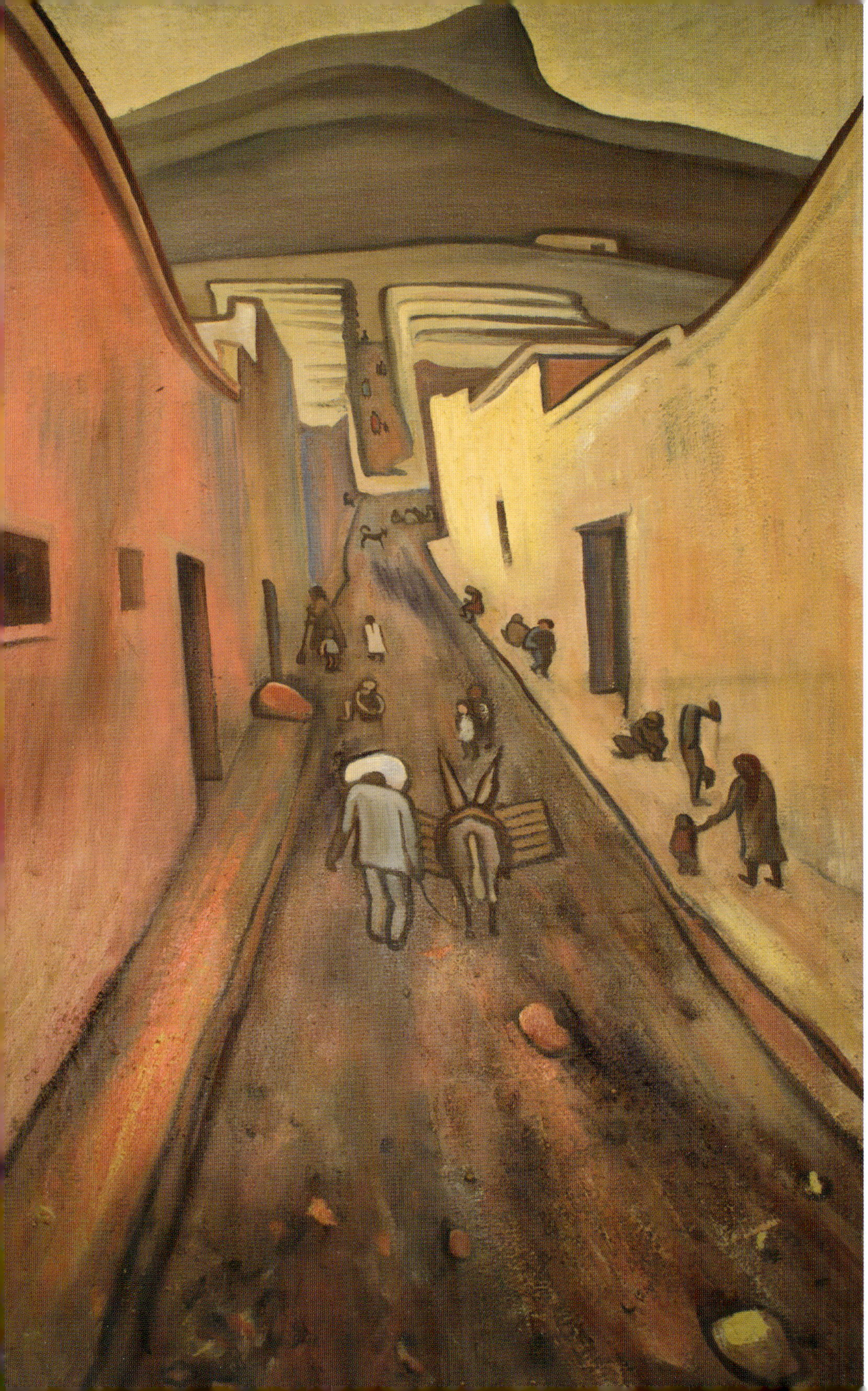

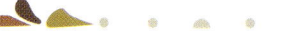

Left:
Don Brown
Street in Saltillo, Mexico, c. 1920-1959
Oil on canvas
Meadows Museum of Art
Stein Collection of Don Brown Works

Opposite:
Don Brown
Mexican Village Street, c. 1920-1959
Watercolor on paper
Meadows Museum of Art
Stein Collection of Don Brown Works

Painter Don Brown spent considerable time in both Louisiana and Mexico, helping to shape Louisiana art both through his work as an artist in New Orleans and as a longtime professor of art at Centenary College in Shreveport. Brown was well known throughout the South for his paintings and charcoals, which reflect the influence of his artistic training in Texas as well as his time spent living and working in both Louisiana and Mexico.

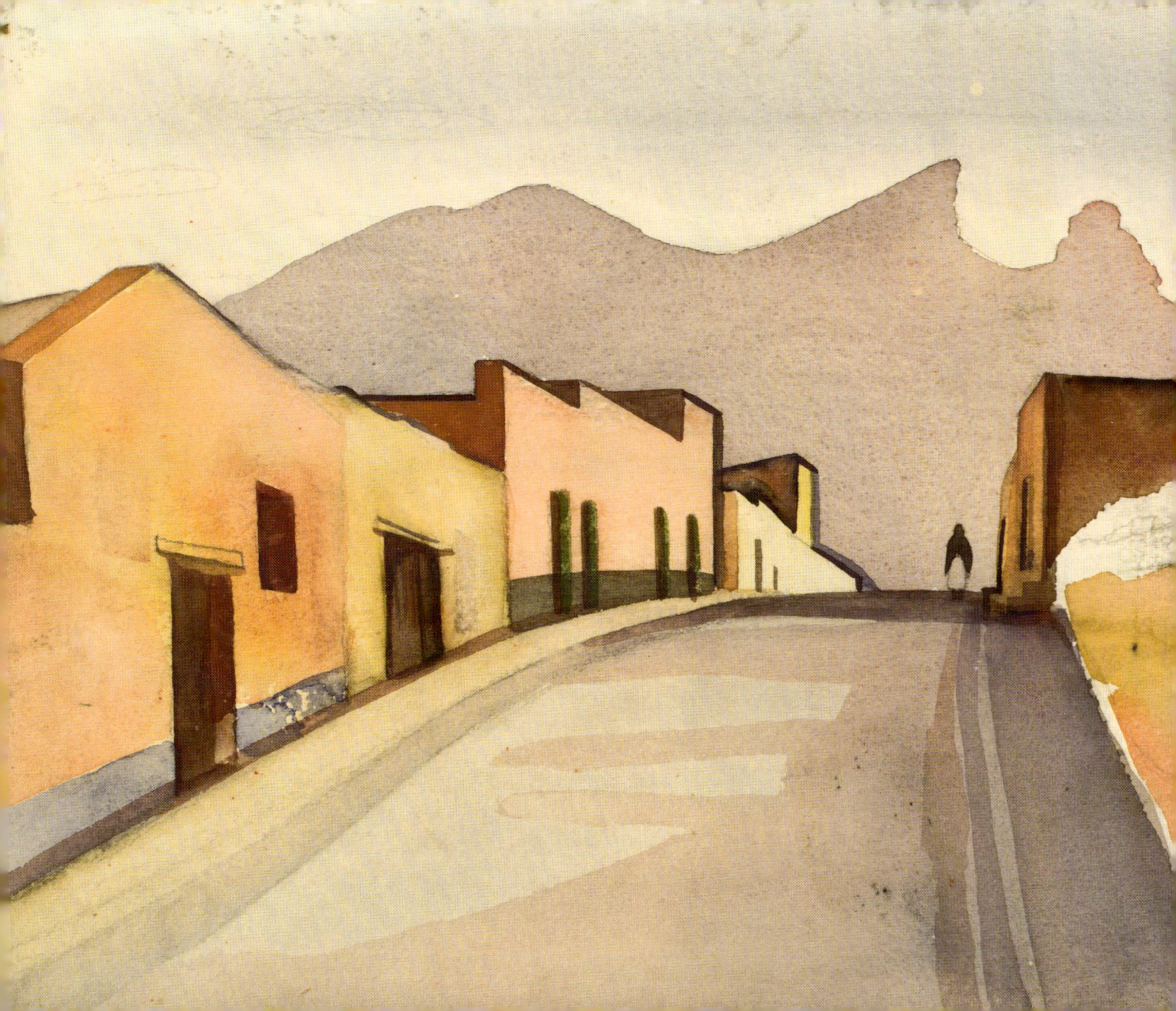

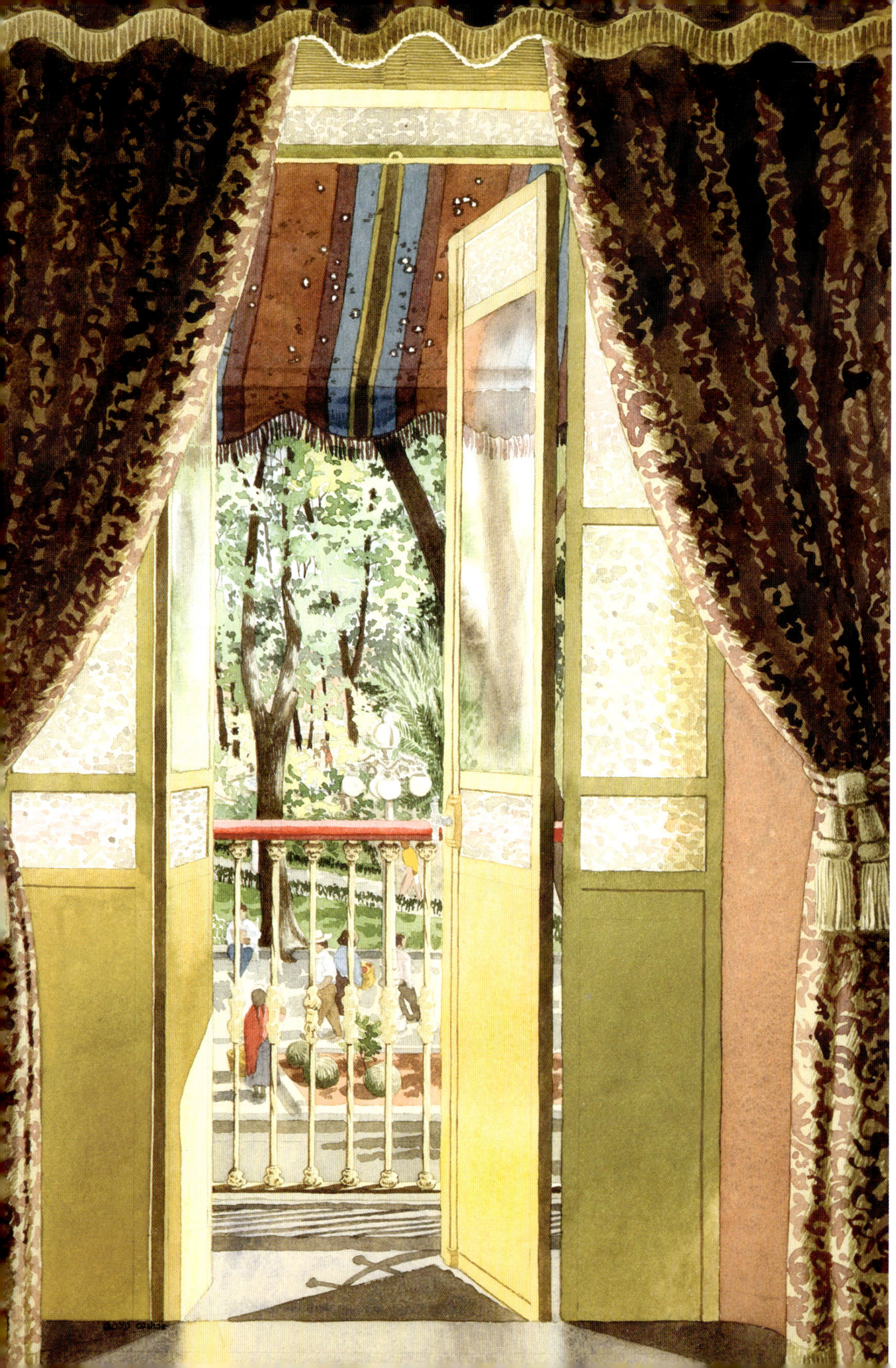

BOYD CRUISE
Mexican Square, 1979
Watercolor on board
The Historic New Orleans Collection, 1997.90
Gift of Mr. and Mrs. Fred Smith

Boyd Cruise's romantic watercolor paintings of New Orleans reflect his deep love for the city and its storied architectural history. His meticulous renderings of French Quarter scenes showcase his passion for the city's architecture, which he saw as closely related to the architecture of South and Central America. Originally from Mississippi, Cruise studied at the Pennsylvania Academy of Fine Arts, and his paintings of New Orleans often portray the place as an exotic locale more closely tied with South America and Europe than the United States. Like many New Orleans artists, Cruise frequently visited Mexico throughout the 1940s through 1980s. His paintings of Mexico, like his work in New Orleans, often emphasized the bright colors and vibrant shapes and forms of Mexican architecture, and stood in stark contrast to the more staid modern architectural forms in concrete and steel increasingly to be found in northeastern cities like Philadelphia.

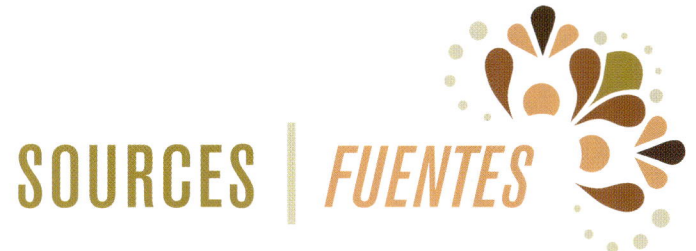

SOURCES | *FUENTES*

[1]Leslie Byrd Simpson, "Introduction" from Stuart Chase, *Mexico: A Study of Two Americas* (New York: The Macmillan Company, 1942).

[2]See Ramon Eduardo Ruiz, *The Great Rebellion, Mexico 1905-1924* (New York: W. W. Norton & Company, 1980) and John S. D. Eisenhower, *Intervention! The United States and the Mexican Revolution, 1913-1917* (New York: W. W. Norton and Company, 1995).

[3]Frances Toor, "Homenaje a Diego Rivera/ Tribute to Diego Rivera," *Mexican Folkways* 1930, Volume 6, No. 4, The Latin American Library at Tulane Special Collections, L972 398.05 M611 1930 no. 4

[4]Robert L. Brunhouse, *Frans Blom: Maya Explorer* (Albuquerque: University of New Mexico Press, 1996), p. 61. After a 1925 expedition, Blom boasted to a New Orleans newspaper that he had "discovered 24 ruined cities hitherto unknown."

[5]Spratling first visited Mexico in 1926, and travelled between New Orleans and Mexico throughout the 1920s before setting up permanent residence in Taxco to start his silver design business. See Taylor D. Littleton, *Wiliam Spratling: His Life and Art* (Baton Rouge: Lousiana State University Press, 2000).

[6]See Penny C. Morrill, *Modern Silver: Modern Handwrought Jewelry and Metalwork* (Lancaster: Schiffer Publishing Limited, 2007) and Penny C. Morrill, *Silver Masters of Mexico, Hector Aguilar and the Taller Borda* (Lancaster: Schiffer Publishing Limited, 1997).

[7]As quoted in Littleton, *Wiliam Spratling: His Life and Art*, p. 225.

[8]See William Spratling, *Little Mexico* (New York: Jonathan, Cape & Harrison Smith, 1932)

[9]William Spratling, "13 Woodcuts by Siqueiros," in David Alfaro Siqueiros, *13 Grabados en Madera por Siqueiros, Taxco,* 1931 (printed 1992), Portfolio of 13 woodcuts (12 printed on orange paper and one printed on lavender paper), The Latin American Library at Tulane Special Collections, Spratling-Taxco Collection, MSS Collection 148.

[10]Selby Noel Mayfield, "Mexican Paintings are Picturesque," *The Times-Picayune,* March 23, 1930, p. 14.

[11]*The Times-Picayune,* March 23, 1930, p. 14.

[12]William Spratling, "Diego Rivera," *Mexican Folkways* 1930, Volume VI, No. 4, pp. 162-196, The Latin American Library at Tulane Special Collections, L972 398.05 M611 1930, no. 4.

[13]Diego Rivera, "Mexican Painting: The Portrait," *Mexican Folkways,* February-March 1926, Vol. 1, No. 5, The Latin American Library at Tulane Special Collections, L972 398.05 M611 1925/1926.

[14]*The Times-Picayune,* October 17, 1927, p. 19.

[15]*The Times-Picayune,* October 14, 1928, p. 27.

[16]Selby Noel Mayfield, "Mexican Paintings are Picturesque," *The Times Picayune,* March 23, 1930, p. 14.

[17]*The Times-Picayune,* November 12, 1933, p. 21.

[18]"Carrie Durieux," wrote Leonhardt from Mexico, "sent her portrait that [Rivera] did of her when she lived here…this is the third time that I've seen it shown [here]." See Olive Leonhardt, *Letter from the Hotel Maria Cristina,* August 3, 1949, Olive Leonhardt Correspondence, Collection of Gay Leonhardt; See also "Work of Mexican Artists," *The Times Picayune,* February 20, 1946, p. 26. "Diego Rivera's 'Portrait of Caroline Durieux," the article writes, "is the most striking feature of the show, excluding the various 'repeat' exhibits. The self-portrait is by the artist's former wife Frida Kahlo, rimmed with parrots, is also of interest."

[19]See Ariel Zuñiga, *Emilio Amero: Un Modernista Liminal/A Liminal Modernist* (Mexico: Albedrio, 2008).

[20]Diego Rivera, "On the Work of Caroline Durieux," *Mexican Folkways* 1929, Volume 5, No. 3, The Latin American Library at Tulane Special Collections L927 (398.05) M611 1929 Vol. 5, No. 3.

[21]"Caroline Durieux Art Exhibition," *El Universal Anglo-American,* June 10, 1934, Folder 7, Box 3, Caroline Wogan Durieux Papers, MSS 3827, LSU Libraries Special Collections; Untitled article from *El Excelsior,* Mexico City, October 1929, Folder 7, Box 3, Caroline Wogan Durieux Papers, MSS 3827, LSU Libraries Special Collections.

[22]Diego Rivera, "Caroline Durieux," *Mexican Folkways,* 1935, The Latin American Library at Tulane Special Collections, L972 398.05 M611 1933/1935.

[23]Diego Rivera, "Caroline Durieux," *Mexican Folkways,* 1929, Vol. 5, No. 4, The Latin American Library at Tulane Special Collections, L927 398.05 M611 1929 Vol. 5, No. 4.

[24]*The Times-Picayune,* February 16, 1936, p. 21.

[25]"Society Page," *New Orleans Item,* November 20, 1921, p. 41.

[26]Daisy Weinberg, "She Tells New Orleans Painters to Paint New Orleans Things," *New Orleans Item,* November 16, 1931.

[27]Ibid.

[28]Originally from Chicago, Morris Henry Hobbs settled in New Orleans in 1938 after a sketching trip to the Vieux Carre left him enchanted by the city's architecture. His "Old New Orleans" series of prints of the French Quarter earned him national acclaim as an etcher. Hobbs visited central Mexico in the early 1940s. *See* Claudia Kate Kheel, *Morris Henry Hobbs: Printmaker, 1892-1967,* M.A. Thesis, Tulane University, 1994.

[29]Frances Toor, "Homenaje a Diego Rivera/ Tribute to Diego Rivera," *Mexican Folkways* 1930, Volume 6, No. 4, The Latin American Library at Tulane Special Collections, L972 398.05 M611 1930 no. 4.

[30]Melanie Anne Herzog, *Elizabeth Catlett: An American Artist in Mexico* (Seattle: University of Washington Press, 2000), 70.

[31]See *Enrique Alferez: Art and Life,* ex. cat., Ogden Museum of Art, 2002.

[32]*The Times-Picayune,* January 30, 1933, p. 11.

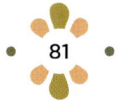

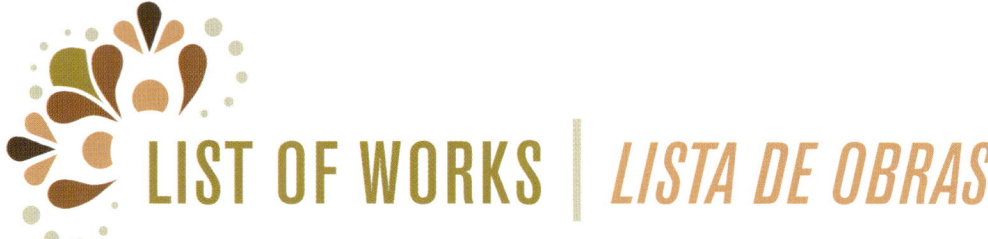

LIST OF WORKS | *LISTA DE OBRAS*

Conrad A. Albrizio

Seated Mexican Peasant, 1947
Pencil on paper
LSU Museum of Art, 93.17.3
Gift of Dr. and Mrs. Robert B. Smythe

Untitled (Mexican Scene), u.d.
Watercolor on paper
LSU Museum of Art, 2006.8.2
Gift of Mrs. Janice Sachse; Transfer from the
West Baton Rouge Historical Association

Enrique Alferez

Drawing of a Man, 1940
Crayon on orange paper
The Historic New Orleans Collection, 1968.12.1
Gift of Mr. Albert L. Lieutaud

Study for Dancers, c. 1990s
Crayon on paper
Collection of Dr. Tlaloc Alferez

Dancers, c. 1990s
2 Carved mohogany panels
Collection of Dr. Tlaloc Alferez

Emilio Amero

*Girl Combing her Hair (Muchacha
peinandose)*, 1950
Color lithographic ink on warm rag paper
Meadows Museum of Art
Stein Collection of Don Brown Works

*The Florence Cane Daughters (Las Hijas
de Florence Cane)*, 1936
Lithograph in red, green, yellow, blue and
black on cream wove paper
Meadows Museum of Art
Stein Collection of Don Brown Works

The Gesture (El Gesto), 1948
Lithograph on paper
Meadows Museum of Art
Stein Collection of Don Brown Works

Where? Donde?, 1929-1950
Color lithographic ink on warm white rag paper
Meadows Museum of Art
Stein Collection of Don Brown Works

Woman with Rebozo (Mujer con rebozo), 1938
Lithograph in red, yellow, blue and black
inks on white paper
Meadows Museum of Art
Stein Collection of Don Brown Works

Don Brown

Mexican Village Street, c. 1920-1959
Watercolor on paper
Meadows Museum of Art
Stein Collection of Don Brown Works

Street in Saltillo, Mexico, c. 1920-1959
Oil on canvas
Meadows Museum of Art
Stein Collection of Don Brown Works

Chato Castillo

Azteca Parrot Brooch, 1953
Silver
Collection of Penny Morrill

Los Castillo

Album Page with Jewelry Designs, u.d.
Ink and watercolor on paper
The Latin American Library, Tulane University
Spratling-Taxco Collection

Los Castillo Silver Pitcher with Bird, c. 1950s
Silver with green turquoise
Collection of Shanna Boudreaux

Margot Van Voorhies Castillo

Los Castillo Ce Acatl Necklace, c. 1939-40
Silver
Collection of Penny Morrill

Elizabeth Catlett

I have always worked hard in America, 1946
(printed 1989)
Linocut
The Historic New Orleans Collection, 2013.0222.2
Acquisition made possible by the Laussat Society

I have given the world my songs, 1947
(printed 1989)
Linocut
The Historic New Orleans Collection,
2013.0222.5
Acquisition made possible by the Laussat Society

...In the Fields, 1947 (printed 1989)
Linocut
The Historic New Orleans Collection,
2013.0222.3
Acquisition made possible by the Laussat Society

[Male] Sharecropper, 1945
Woodcut
The Historic New Orleans Collection,
2014.0077.3

*My role has been important to the struggle to
organize the unorganized*, 1947 (printed 1989)
Linocut
The Historic New Orleans Collection,
2013.0222.9
Acquisition made possible by the Laussat Society

Peones Mexicano, 1945 and 47
Linocut
The Historic New Orleans Collection,
2014.0077.5

Sharecropper, 1952 (printed 1968),
2014.0077.1
Color linocut on cream Japanese paper
The Historic New Orleans Collection

...Special houses..., 1946 (printed 1989)
Linocut
The Historic New Orleans Collection,
2013.0222.12
Acquisition made possible by the Laussat Society

*There are bars between me and the rest of the
land...*, 1946 (printed 1989)
Linocut
The Historic New Orleans Collection,
2013.0222.10
Acquisition made possible by the Laussat Society

Young Mexican Girl, Nina, 1945-1947
Color serigraph
The Historic New Orleans Collection,
2014.0077.6

Faye Creations

"Fiesta" Dress, c. 1940s
Black fabric trimmed with brocade
LSU Textile and Costume Museum,
1992.010.0001
Gift of Caroline Wogan Durieux

Boyd Cruise

721 Royal Street, 1946
Watercolor on paper
LSU Museum of Art, 89.9
Gift of the Friends of LSU Museum of Art

Casa de los Munecos/House of Dolls, 1954
Watercolor on paper
The Historic New Orleans Collection, 1956.20

Mexican Flowers in a Banana Stalk, 1979
Watercolor on paper
The Historic New Orleans Collection,
1996.116.2
Gift of Mr. and Mrs. G. Henry Pierson, Jr.

Mexican Square, 1979
Watercolor on board
The Historic New Orleans Collection, 1997.90
Gift of Mr. and Mrs. Fred Smith

Red Plums, 1949
Watercolor on paper
LSU Museum of Art, 85.24
Gift of Milton J. Womack in memory of his wife,
Barbara Sevier Womack

Caroline Wogan Durieux

An Intellectual, 1932
Graphite on paper
Collection of Ann Wilkinson

Bather, 1932
Lithograph on paper
LSU Museum of Art, 68.9.6
Gift of the Artist

Benediction, 1932
Lithograph on paper
LSU Museum of Art, 68.9.2
Gift of the Artist

Bipeds Dancing, 1932
Lithograph on paper
LSU Museum of Art, 68.9.3
Gift of the Artist

Café Tupinamba, 1934
Oil on canvas
LSU Museum of Art, 91.25
Gift of Mr. Charles P. Manship, Jr.; Conservation
with funds provided by Ms. Nadine Carter
Russell

Cartoon Drawing for Café Tupinamba, c. 1934
Lithograph on paper
LSU Museum of Art, 91.26
Gift of the Friends of LSU Museum of Art

Dressmaking, 1932
Lithograph on paper
LSU Museum of Art, 68.9.4
Gift of the Artist

In the French Quarter, New Orleans, 1945
Black lithograph on paper
LSU Museum of Art,68.9.29
Gift of the Artist

Los Diplomáticos, 1942
Lithograph on paper
LSU Museum of Art, 68.9.20
Gift of the Artist

Priests, 1932
Lithograph on paper
LSU Museum of Art, 68.9.1
Gift of the Artist

Survivor, 1947
Black and white lithograph on paper
LSU Museum of Art, 68.9.48
Gift of the Artist

Teatro, 1971
Black and white cliché verre
LSU Museum of Art, 76.12.2
Gift of Caroline Durieux and Mrs. Frank Woody

Viggo A. Hanson

Courtyard, Merida, Yucatan, 1916
Oil on canvas
Collection of John Ed Bradley

Colette Pope Heldner

New Orleans Arts and Crafts Club, 1932
Oil on canvas
Colllection of Don Fuson

Morris Henry Hobbs

Calle de Arco
Etching on paper
The Latin American Library, Tulane University
Reed Isbell Collection of Morris Henry Hobbs
Etchings of Mexico

Calle de Guadalupe, Taxco, Mexico, 1942
Etching on paper
LSU Museum of Art, MOA 10.205.23
Gift of Dr. A. Brooks Cronan, Jr. and Diana
Cronan

Iron Lace, 1949
Etching on paper
Private Collection

Old Church Doorway Taxco, Mexico, 1942
Drypoint etching on paper
The Latin American Library, Tulane University
Reed Isbell Collection of Morris Henry Hobbs
Etchings of Mexico

Patio of the Bosque House, Old New Orleans,
1945
Etching on Paper
Private Collection

Pirates Alley, Old New Orleans, 1943
Etching on paper
Private Collection

Plazuela Bernal, Taxco, Mexico, 1942
Drypoint etching on paper
The Latin American Library, Tulane University
Reed Isbell Collection of Morris Henry Hobbs
Etchings of Mexico

Plazuela Bernal, Taxco, Mexico, 1942
Graphite drawing on cream paper
The Latin American Library, Tulane University
Reed Isbell Collection of Morris Henry Hobbs
Etchings of Mexico

Olive Leonhardt

Blessed Virgin Returns to the Fiesta, c.
1935-39
Oil on canvas
Collection of Gay Leonhardt

Calla Manana, c. 1935-39
Oil on canvas
Collection of Gay Leonhardt

Convent of the Holy Family, New Orleans, c.
1935-39
Oil on board
Collection of Gay Leonhardt

Journey to the End of Night, c. 1935-39
Oil on canvas
Collection of Gay Leonhardt

Oaxaca Boy, c. 1930s
Oil on board
Collection of Gay Leonhardt

Orizaba Girl, c. 1930s
Oil on board
Collection of Gay Leonhardt

Orizaba Man, c. 1930s
Oil on board
Collection of Gay Leonhardt

*Preparatory sketch for Blessed Virgin Returns
to the Fiesta*, c. 1935-39
Pastel on paper
Collection of Gay Leonhardt

Shopping, c. 1935-39
Oil on board
Collection of Gay Leonhardt

The Tomb, c. 1935-39
Oil on canvas
Collection of Gay Leonhardt

Woman with Lilies, c. 1935-39
Oil on board
Collection of Gay Leonhardt

Charles Oglesby Longabaugh

Spratling y Artesanos, u.d.
Watercolor on paper
The Latin American Library, Tulane University
Spratling-Taxco Collection

Clarence Millet

French Quarter Scene, c. 1930
Oil on canvas
LSU Museum of Art, 2006.7.10
Gift of the Friends of LSU Libraries
Transfer from LSU Libraries' Special Collections

Edward Millman

Mexico Series, 1935
Pastel and watercolor on paper
LSU Museum of Art, L2015.4.77
Gift of Mark and Catherine K. Potter and the
Paula G. Manship Museum of Art Endowment
for Acquisition and Conservation

Bayou Nutria Series, c. 1946
Pastel and watercolor on paper
Gift of Mark and Catherine K. Potter and the
Paula G. Manship Museum of Art Endowment
for Acquisition and Conservation

Diego Rivera

Mexican Flower Market, 1930
Lithograph on paper
Private Collection

Portrait of Caroline Durieux, 1929
Oil on canvas
LSU Museum of Art, 2000.2
Gift of Paula Garvey Manship

Carlos Orozco Romero

Portrait of Caroline Durieux, 1928
Watercolor on heavy paper
LSU Museum of Art, 74.1.3
Gift of Caroline Wogan Durieux

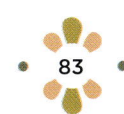

David Alfaro Siqueiros

13 Grabados en Madera por Siqueiros, Taxco, 1931 (printed 1992)
Portfolio of 13 woodcuts (12 printed on orange paper and one printed on lavender paper)
The Latin American Library, Tulane University
Spratling-Taxco Collection

"Spratling," u.d.
Lithograph on paper
The Latin American Library, Tulane University
Spratling-Taxco Collection

William Spratling

2 Campeche Chairs, c. 1930s
Wood and leather
Collection of Caroline Wogan Sontheimer and Stephen Louis Sontheimer

Acuitlapan, u.d.
Ink and charcoal on white paper
The Latin American Library, Tulane University
Spratling-Taxco Collection

Aztec Sun Brooch, c. 1940
Silver
Collection of Penny Morrill

Bird Ashtray, c. 1940s
Silver
Collection of Don Fuson

Candlesticks, c. 1940s
Wood and silver
Collection of Don Fuson

Coffee Table, c. 1940s
Wood and leather
Collection of Don Fuson

Cream Pitcher, c. 1931-45
Sterling silver and rosewood
LSU Museum of Art, 96.10
Gift of the Friends of LSU Museum of Art

Double Bird Brooch, c. 1937
Silver
Collection of Penny Morrill

Hands Across America Brooch, 1942
Silver
Collection of Penny Morrill

Maguey, u.d.
Ink and charcoal on white paper
The Latin American Library, Tulane University
Spratling-Taxco Collection

Necklace Design, c. 1940
Ink and watercolor on onion skin paper
The Latin American Library, Tulane University
Spratling-Taxco Collection

Necklace Design, u.d.
Ink and watercolor on onion skin paper
The Latin American Library, Tulane University
Spratling-Taxco Collection

Original Necklace Design for a Long Triple Jade Pendant with Three Gold Balls, c. 1955-1967
Ink and watercolor on paper
The Latin American Library, Tulane University
Spratling-Taxco Collection

Owl Brooch, c. 1940
Silver with amethyst quartz cabochons
Collection of Penny Morrill

Petate brooch, c. 1940
Silver
Collection of Penny Morrill

Parrot Brooch, c. 1940
Silver with amethyst cabochon
Collection of Penny Morrill

Pre-Columbian Clay Seal Stamp Imprints 22-28, u.d.
Photostatic copy on paper
The Latin American Library, Tulane University
Spratling-Taxco Collection

Pre-Columbian Clay Seal Stamp Imprints 107-115, u.d.
Photostatic copy on paper
The Latin American Library, Tulane University
Spratling-Taxco Collection

Quetzalcoatl brooch, c. 1940
Silver
Collection of Penny Morrill

Silver Boxes, c. 1940s
Silver and tortoiseshell
Collection of Don Fuson

Silver Pitchers, c. 1940s
Silver
Collection of Don Fuson

Silver Tray, c. 1940s
Silver with amethyst quartz cabochons
Collection of Don Fuson

Sun and Moon Brooch, c. 1940
Silver with copper wash
Collection of Penny Morrill

The Garden Gate, u.d.
Ink and charcoal on white paper
The Latin American Library, Tulane University
Spratling-Taxco Collection

Wood and Silver Bowl, c. 1940s
Wood and silver
Collection of Don Fuson

J.F. Swalley

Street in Guanajuato, u.d.
Etching on cream paper
The Latin American Library, Tulane University
Reed Isbell Collection of Morris Henry Hobbs
Etchings of Mexico

James Swann

Street in Taxco, to Morris Henry Hobbs, u.d.
Etching on paper
The Latin American Library, Tulane University
Reed Isbell Collection of Morris Henry Hobbs
Etchings of Mexico

Ruffino Tamayo

Illustrations from the Apocalypse de Saint, 1959
Color lithographic ink on warm, handmade paper
Meadows Museum of Art

Unknown Artist

Mexican Modernist Rug, c. 1930s
Woven wool
Collection of H. P. and Barbara Bacot

Photograph of William Spratling Holding a Design Album, u.d.
Gelatin silver print
The Latin American Library, Tulane University
Spratling-Taxco Collection

Photograph of William Spratling Holding one of his Candlesticks, c. 1940s
Gelatin silver print
The Latin American Library, Tulane University
Spratling-Taxco Collection

Photograph of the Los Castillos Store in Taxco, Mexico, c. 1940s
Gelatin silver print
The Latin American Library, Tulane University
Spratling-Taxco Collection

Photograph of William Spratling's Studio in Taxco, Mexico, c. 1940s
Gelatin silver print
The Latin American Library, Tulane University
Spratling-Taxco Collection

Precolumbian Tripod Vessel with human feet, c. 500-1200
Painted ceramic vessel

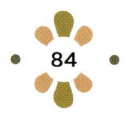